Accountability in Syria

Accountability in Syria

Achieving Transitional Justice in a Postconflict Society

**Edited by
Radwan Ziadeh**

LEXINGTON BOOKS
Lanham • Boulder • New York • London

Published by Lexington Books
An imprint of The Rowman & Littlefield Publishing Group, Inc.
4501 Forbes Boulevard, Suite 200, Lanham, Maryland 20706
www.rowman.com

6 Tinworth Street, London SE11 5AL

British Library Cataloguing in Publication Information Available

Library of Congress Control Number: 2019950455
ISBN 978-1-4985-1189-6 (cloth)
ISBN 978-1-4985-1191-9 (pbk)
ISBN 978-1-4985-1190-2 (electronic)

Contents

Special Thanks

The editor would like to express his special gratitude and appreciation to the Arab Center for Research and Policy Studies in Doha for its generous support to do this research and make this book available to the public.

Introduction

Radwan Ziadeh

Since the uprising erupted in Syria in March 2011, the number of the civilians killed exceeds half a million, and more than 6.5 million refugees have fled to Turkey, Jordan, Lebanon, Iraq, and Egypt. At least 7.6 million Syrians have been forced to abandon their homes due to the violence and are internally displaced inside Syria. According to the Independent International Commission of Inquiry on Syria, "Government forces and affiliated militia have committed murder, torture, rape, forcible displacement, enforced disappearance and other inhumane acts." Gross violations of international human rights law—including summary execution, arbitrary arrest and detention, unlawful attack, attacking protected objects, and pillaging and destruction of property—have also been committed.

Syrian government forces have routinely bombarded densely populated civilian areas with artillery, deployed snipers and helicopters in urban areas, and tortured detained protestors and human rights activists. All of these acts are considered crimes against humanity as defined by the Rome Statute that established the International Criminal Court (ICC) in 2002.

Therefore, it is not possible to start a genuine process of transitional justice or a process of political transition toward pluralism, democracy, and reconciliation in Syria without a complete cessation of violence. As transitional justice experiences across the world have demonstrated, reconciliation is closely linked to the path of political transition, and depends primarily on the political will and vision of both the actors and the political forces on the ground. The launching of transitional justice processes will signal to the victims that those responsible for committing crimes against their children will be brought to justice and that the time of impunity is over.

One possible pathway to overcome these obstacles in launching a transitional justice system is resorting to international justice, because the war

crimes and crimes against humanity committed by Assad are certainly within
the scope of work of the International Criminal Court. However, given Russia's position in the UN Security Council, Moscow may prevent the referral
of Syrian criminals to the court. Any future government formed by the opposition or formed post-Assad regime should ratify the Rome agreement in
order to enable a prosecutor to open an investigation into these crimes. The
path of international justice is certainly not an ideal choice; it is too slow,
particularly because Syrian victims need their rights guaranteed and not ignored by political compromises. Therefore, it seems that holding hybrid
courts is the best option for Syria and Syrians.

This book will look into the patterns of crimes and crimes against humanity committed in Syria during the conflict, the possibilities to achieve accountability through the international system, the options in front of the
Syrians and the international community, and the linkages between the transition government and the new justice system that should emerge in Syria.

Chapter One

Transition, Justice, and Accountability in Syria

Radwan Ziadeh

Syria became the place where the most serious war crimes and crimes against humanity were perpetrated, even one day the former secretary general Ban Ki-Moon described of what happened in Aleppo as "acronym to Hill."[1] The challenges facing the international human rights, and justice communities are vast, as impunity has become the new culture and the circle of violence has turned out to be the only reality. The UN Commission of Inquiry documented the patterns of the crimes in Syria, and concluded that the crimes include "everyday war crimes and crimes against Humanity."[2] The widespread brutality of such crimes requires a response from the international community beyond condemnations and statements.

The Syrian conflict has now entered its eighth year. Violence has displaced millions and killed at least 600,000. Many Syrian cities, towns, and neighborhoods, like Daraya, Madayia, and Al-Moudamia, have been destroyed or abandoned. The fabric of Syrian society has been torn to shreds.

A HISTORY OF VIOLENCE

As in other states that have considered conducting transitional justice programs, Syria has a long history of regime-sponsored human rights violations. Emergency law remained in effect in Syria from 1963 to 2011. During that time (and to this day), the government strictly limited freedom of expression, assembly, and association, and harassed and imprisoned human rights defenders and nonviolent critics of government policies.[3] According to Human Rights Watch, "Syria has a long record of arbitrary arrests, systematic torture, prolonged detention of suspects, and grossly unfair trials."[4] Political arrests and forced disappearances became systemic and continuous during the late 1970s and early 1980s, coinciding with the outbreak of violent conflict between the Muslim Brotherhood and the Syrian regime. The regime started using unmitigated violence not only against armed Islamist organizations but also against the entire spectrum of opposition parties and their supporters in Syrian society. This culminated in a number of massacres that killed thousands of civilians, most notably the massacre of Hama in February 1982. The assassination attempt on then President Hafez al-Assad was followed by the massacre of Palmyra on June 27, 1980, in which hundreds of detainees were shot at the notorious military prison. Human rights groups estimate that about 1,000 victims were buried in unknown mass graves.

Since the uprising erupted in Syria in March 2011, the number of arrests and enforced disappearances has increased dramatically. According to the Syrian Network for Human Rights, an estimated 215,000 individuals have been arrested in Syria in the last six years. Of those, the network estimates that some 60,000 have been forcibly disappeared. Unfortunately, these numbers are difficult to verify as families of victims often refuse to speak to human rights violation investigators out of fear for their imprisoned relatives' lives.[5]

Additionally, regime-propagated violence and clashes between the Syrian army and rebel forces have resulted in the deaths of 450,000 people and laid waste to the country. More than 6.5 million refugees have fled to Turkey, Jordan, Lebanon, Iraq, and Egypt. At least 7.6 million Syrians have been forced to abandon their homes due to the violence and are internally displaced inside Syria. According to the Independent International Commission of Inquiry on Syria, "Government forces and affiliated militia have committed murder, torture, rape, forcible displacement, enforced disappearance and other inhumane acts." Gross violations of international human rights law—including summary execution, arbitrary arrest and detention, unlawful attack, attacking protected objects, and pillaging and destruction of property—have also been committed.[6]

Syrian government forces have routinely bombarded densely populated civilian areas with artillery, deployed snipers and helicopters in urban areas, and tortured detained protestors and human rights activists. All of these acts are considered crimes against humanity as defined by the Rome Statute that established the International Criminal Court (ICC) in 2002.

THE MAPPING OF THE CONFLICT IN SYRIA

The situation in Syria continues to defy an observer's understanding of reality. Indeed, no Syrian in 2011 imagined that Syria would be like it is today. The brutality of the Syrian regime of Bashar al-Assad defies imagination, and at the same time Syrian society had high expectations that the international community would help them not to allow a scenario of war crimes and crimes against humanity to unfold in their country.

Starting in 2013, the Assad regime's barrel bombs started raining down on the population and became the most systematic and widespread weapon the government used against civilians. By July 2015, as areas in Syria were no longer under government control, more than 120,000 people lost their lives due to barrel bombs.[7] The response of the international community was to ignore this grave violation of international humanitarian law (IHL).

Again, the Assad government used sarin gas in August 2013,[8] killing more than 1,000 people and bringing the total number of casualties from chemical attacks in Syria to 1,500 as of March 2016. Again, the Syrian government stated that it had given up its arsenal of chemical weapons after the deal between the United States, under the Obama Administration, and Russia in 2013. Nevertheless, the government brazenly used sarin gas again in April 2017,[9] leaving at least 83 dead in Khan Sheikhoun in Idlib province. The Syrian American Medical Society has documented 109 chlorine gas attacks in Syria since the civil war began in 2011.[10]

In 2016 and 2017 we witnessed different types of violations of IHL, which included the enforced transfer of part of the population against its will.

The population swap deal came after five different and earlier deals that included Sunni cities that participated in anti-government protests in 2011. Their populations then joined the armed opposition to defend their towns and prevent Syrian government troops from invading or entering them and massacring the civilians. International organizations reported that these displacement deals had been perpetrated based on sectarian lines.

The first city that was subject to such an enforced displacement deal was Homs.[11] The neighborhoods of the old city, which are predominantly Sunni, were subjected to massive shelling and near-total destruction, forcing most of their people to flee.

This agreement led to emptying the old town completely of its native inhabitants in order to attract more loyalists to the government. The population of Homs dropped from 1.5 million in 2011 to nearly 400,000 people today, with 65 percent of the city's indigenous population leaving to Idlib province.

The Darayya massacre of August 2012, where more than 700 civilians were slaughtered, led to increased recruitment for the Free Syrian Army (FSA) in the town. The FSA took full control of the city in 2014. Due to its closeness to the capital, Damascus, the Assad government encircled Darayya and put it under a brutal siege with no access to food or water. The civilians remaining in the town came to depend completely on the underground tunnel network for almost four years; they endured heavy bombardment, including barrel bombs, nearly every day. The United Nations' Under-Secretary-Gen-

eral for Humanitarian Affairs and Emergency Relief Coordinator, Stephen
O'Brien, actually called Darayya "Syria's capital of barrel bombs."[12] Eventually the civilians and militants decided to give up after threats from the
government in 2016 that it would burn what was left of the city; the civilians
fled to Idlib, which became the capital of the opposition.

Darayya, a city whose population was 250,000 before 2011, became empty. For almost four years its inhabitants were deprived of medical and food
aid. The only UN convoy allowed by the government to enter the city since
2012 entered on June 10, 2016, when a delegation of UN officials along with
essential assistance distributed contraceptive pills and mosquito-resistant
tents, which they said was what the government allowed. The government
then bombarded the town with tens of barrel bombs and the United Nations
did not try to bring aid to Darayya again. After the completion of the forced
displacement of the city's inhabitants, President Assad made a rare trip to the
empty city in September 2016 and performed the Eid al-Adha prayer in a
mosque there.[13] He responded (AR) to a journalist's question about the demographic changes in Syria by saying that a city's demography "changes
across generations" and pointing out that this is based on the interests of
citizens in those areas. He added, "As for Syria, as in any country, the
demographic situation is changing because of the economic benefit of the
people, the social status and the political conditions vary. Of course, I do not
talk about the countryside. The villages are different, but the cities are always
diverse, being close to major cities like Damascus and Aleppo are diverse
cities that can't be of one color and one form."

In examining these events, it is clear that Assad refused to mention one
critical component of his strategy: that all civilians in Darayya were evacuated into Idlib against their will. Those who decided not to leave were then at
the regime's mercy and were detained or tortured; others were bussed into
rebel areas of northern Syria in a forced population transfer. During the
negotiations, the government secured concessions by threatening to kill all
civilians unless rebels left the town. This is a clear violation of IHL and can
be seen as a sign of ethnic cleansing and demographic change that has resulted from the Syrian conflict.

Rule 129[14] of the Customary IHL states clearly that "Parties to a non-
international armed conflict may not order the displacement of the civilian
population, in whole or in part, for reasons related to the conflict, unless the
security of the civilians involved or imperative military reasons so demand."
Further, the Statute of the International Criminal Court states that in non-
international armed conflicts, "ordering the displacement of the civilian population for reasons related to the conflict, unless the security of the civilians
involved or imperative military reasons so demand" constitutes a war crime.

Unfortunately, the events in Homs and then in Darayya in December
2016, which were repeated in Aleppo in early 2017, were carried out by US-

backed moderate local rebels, like those in Darayya. There, too, Russia launched blistering air raids at the start of the Geneva talks in January 2017 to help the regime place 300,000 people under siege. Syrian regime forces, along with Iraqi and Iranian militias backed by Russian air support, used the same tactics that were well documented by the Atlantic Council's investigative experts,[15] such as barrel bombs and other heavy missiles that targeted all hospitals and medical centers, and chlorine gas, which sent a clear message to civilians and militants that they have no other option but to leave their homes and neighborhoods. This strategy worked very well in Aleppo with the support of Turkey and Russia, which brokered the deal and then launched the Astana talks to give it a political cover.

RUSSIA'S ROLE IN SYRIA

In May 2017, Russia, Turkey, and Iran signed an agreement to establish "de-escalation zones"[16] in Syria. Considered the broker of this deal, Russia emphasized that the four declared zones in Syria are not actually "safe zones" but "de-escalation zones," in a further step to distinguish these zones from the concept of safe zones, which had been flooding the conversations about Syria for some time.

This move by Russia is not incidental. There is no legal definition of such "de-escalation zones" in international law. Such terms are used more readily from a military perspective rather than a legal one, making these terms vague and prone to differing definitions and interpretations. This legal ambiguity serves the interests of Russia, which has already been accused by international organizations of war crimes and crimes against humanity in Syria.

The May 2017 agreement and its contents fall in line with Russia's agenda in pushing the Astana talks. Moscow tried hard to push Astana as the venue to discuss the peace process in Syria, thus attempting to delegitimize any UN efforts in Geneva and, more importantly, allowing Russia to select the type of Syrian opposition groups it would like to deal with. Russia, especially after the battle of Aleppo, claimed to focus on imposing the ceasefire all over Syria. Thus, along with Turkey and Iran, it created the Astana negotiations track as a means to enforce the ceasefire since the agreement between Turkey and Russia in 2016.

What is interesting about this ceasefire is that it was not only violated daily by the Assad regime's air force in eastern Ghota and other areas controlled by the opposition, but the entire population of Syrians in the Waer neighborhood in Homs and four other towns—Madaya, Zabadani, Foua, and Kefraya—were forced to leave their homes due to attacks by the Assad government and the government's use of chemical weapons in Khan Sheikhhoon and Idlib. The question here is, if chemical weapons are used in a "ceasefire time," what can be expected in a "non-ceasefire time"? This situation likely decreases the parties' respect for such a deal. Russia, however, denied the reality of the collapse of such a ceasefire and moved to discuss "de-escalation zones" in the last round of the talks in Astana in May 2017.

NO PEACE WITHOUT ACCOUNTABILITY

As a result, the responsibility falls on the post-Assad government (depending on what form this government will take) and Syrian civil society to prosecute those responsible for human rights violations. Therefore, the new United Nations General Assembly (UNGA) resolution is very important because it puts a stone on the long road to justice within an internal and international environment that doesn't welcome justice over stability.

The international community has abandoned Syrians and left them to die at the hands of their government. Indiscriminate aerial bombardment has taken the lives of more than 600,000 civilians so far,[17] and Bashar al-Assad's forces have made extensive use of short-range Scud ballistic missiles— which are classified as vehicles of weapons of mass destruction—against areas of Syria that are no longer under the regime's control, with utter disregard for the lives of Syrian civilians and for the amount of destruction inflicted upon residential areas and infrastructures.[18]

Whether on the national or international level, justice must be sought on behalf of the victims of violent events in Syria. The culture of impunity that lasted for so long in Syria under the government of the Ba`ath Party should end. This is the only way to open the door to national reconciliation efforts carried out through a comprehensive transitional justice process.

The Syrian people will face two options is pursuing justice in the future, the domestic option or the international one, despite the fact that the first one is very slim for many reasons, including a lack of the capacity of the Syrian judiciary; the size of the massive crimes committed in Syria, which are beyond the ability of any small state to handle by itself; and above all the division and polarization that Syrian society is going through today, which makes it difficult or even impossible for any judicial process to get the trust or the confidence of the Syrian people.

But at the same time, the domestic option will be shorter than the international one, the cost of such a process will be far and away cheaper than the internationalized one, and the ability of the victims to be represented within the court system will be higher since the victims will more involved in domestic courts.

Still, there are very serious obstacles to reaching the domestic option due to the fact of the Russian veto at the security council, which prevents any referral of the situation in Syria to the International Criminal Court. Therefore, it looks like this road is blocked, and this is why the only option left is the hybrid international court, which will mix international law with the Syrian law. Such a strategy has been implemented before in Sierra Leone and Cambodia. The structure of such hybrid courts can fit into the model of Syrian courts exactly.

Therefore, it seems that the hybrid courts are the best option for Syria and Syrians. The tribunals will be held on Syrian territory and will involve the direct participation of Syrian judges supported by international expertise, perhaps under the supervision of the United Nations.

The necessity of international involvement is to have assurance that there is no bias or discrimination, as such feeling will be very active in this divided society after the conflict, no matter how the conflict ends.

The international standards of justice and transparency will be guaranteed. The goal is not to target a specific religious or minority group and hold them accountable, but to establish the course of justice that can ensure justice for all without any discrimination based on religion, ethnicity, or race.

In the future, Syria should be a state based on the respect of law and should end impunity for those who committed crimes. This is the only way Syria can gain the trust of the international community, which should help them to build the new system and its commitment to justice and reconciliation. There is no place for the policies of revenge or retaliation within its program.

The last attempt at such a complicated process was the UNGA resolution to establish the International, Impartial and Independent Mechanism (IIIM)[19] for accountability for crimes in Syria (A/71/L.48), which gives hope to Syrians that there will be accountability for the crimes committed against the Syrian people in the last six years.

This new mechanism came after the failure of the UN Security Council to refer these crimes to the International Criminal Court to hold the perpetrators accountable, which is becoming more difficult, especially after the Russian intervention in Syria since September 2015.

But the IIIM process plays the role of collecting evidence rather than assuring accountability, so we still have a long road ahead of us to keep the issue of justice part of any talks or negotiations in Syria. I do believe that such unanswered crimes have stretched Syrian society to the breaking point. And though justice will play a critical role in the Syrian future, prosecutions alone will not guarantee a successful start to the next chapter in Syria's history. Syrian civil society organizations have a responsibility to immediately begin taking steps toward mending Syria's social fabric and encouraging reconciliation and social cohesion.

Syria can overcome the legacy of the past by engaging in a comprehensive national reconciliation, but such a process can achieve its goal only after the conflict is ended and all refugees have returned home; as transitional justice experiences across the world have taught us, reconciliation is closely linked to the path of political transition and depends mainly on the political will and vision of both the actors and the political forces on the ground. Unfortunately, Syria has practically no history of political participation aside from complete domination of the regime-supported Ba`ath Party. This leaves Syria with few options when considering whom to turn to to design and implement post-conflict reconciliation programs.

NOTES

1. Associated Press, "The Latest: US Envoy Wants UN Monitors in Aleppo Quickly," *US News & World Report*, 2016, www.usnews.com/news/world/articles/2016-12-19/the-latest-buses-leave-2-syrian-villages-under-aleppo-deal.

2. The report of the Independent International Commission of Inquiry on the Syrian Arab Republic, which was established on August 22, 2011, by the Human Rights Council through resolution S-17/1, adopted at its 17th special session with a mandate to investigate all alleged violations of international human rights law since March 2011 in the Syrian Arab Republic, see the link http://www.ohchr.org/EN/HRBodies/HRC/IICISyria/Pages/IndependentInternational Commission.aspx.

3. Radwan Ziadeh (ed.), *Years of Fear: The Enforced Disappeared in Syria* (Washington, DC: Transitional Justice Project in the Arab World, 2010); Damascus Center for Human Rights Studies, *Torture in Syria: Shadow Report to Accompany the Syrian Government Initial Report on Measures Taken to Fulfill Its Commitments under the Convention against Torture and Other Cruel, Inhuman or Degrading Treatment or Punishment* (Damascus Center for Human Rights Studies, 2010).

4. "A Wasted Decade," Human Rights Watch, July 16, 2010, http://www.hrw.org/en/node/91580/section/4.

5. Mapping Accountability Efforts in Syria, Public International Law & Policy Group, February 2013, http://www.dchrs.org/english/File/Reports/mapping-accountability-efforts-in-syria.pdf.

6. See all the reports of the Independent International Commission of Inquiry on the Syrian Arab Republic at this link: http://www.ohchr.org/EN/HRBodies/HRC/IICISyria/Pages/IndependentInternationalCommission.aspx.

7. Alessandria Masi, " The Syrian Regime's Barrel Bombs Kill More Civilians Than ISIS And Al Qaeda Combined," *The Times*, August 18, 2015, see the link at http://www.ibtimes.com/syrian-regimes-barrel-bombs-kill-more-civilians-isis-al-qaeda-combined-2057392.

8. Kareem Shaheen, "Almost 1,500 Killed in Chemical Weapons Attacks in Syria," *The Guardian*, March 14, 2016, see the link at https://www.theguardian.com/world/2016/mar/14/syria-chemical-weapons-attacks-almost-1500-killed-report-united-nations.

9. Angela Dewan, Kareem Khadder, and Holly Yan, "Survivors of Syrian Attack Describe Chemical bombs Falling from Sky," *CNN International*, April 6, 2016, see the link at http://www.cnn.com/2017/04/05/middleeast/idlib-syria-attack/.

10. Dorian Geiger, "How Chlorine Gas Became a Weapon in Syria's Civil War," *Aljazeera International*, March 23, 2017, see the link at http://www.aljazeera.com/indepth/features/2017/03/chlorine-gas-weapon-syria-civil-war-170314110043637.html.

11. "Homs: Syrian Revolution's Fallen 'Capital,'" BBC, December 9, 2015, see the link at http://www.bbc.com/news/world-middle-east-15625642.

12. Under-Secretary-General for Humanitarian Affairs and Emergency Relief Coordinator, Stephen O'Brien: Statement to the Security Council on Syria, New York, June 23, 2016, https://reliefweb.int/report/syrian-arab-republic/under-secretary-general-humanitarian-affairs-and-emergency-relief-42.

13. "Syria's Bashar Al-Assad Prays in Daraya Mosque for Eid Al-Adha," NBC News, September 12, 2016, www.nbcnews.com/news/world/syria-s-bashar-al-assad-prays-daraya-mosque-eid-al-n646566.

14. Rule 129, The Act of Displacement, https://ihl-databases.icrc.org/customary-ihl/eng/docs/v1_rul_rule129.

15. Ben Nimmo et al., "Breaking Aleppo," Atlantic Council, 2017, www.atlanticcouncil.org/publications/reports/breaking-aleppo.

16. Bassem Mroue and Zeina Karam, "Russia, Iran, Turkey Sign on 'de-Escalation Zones' in Syria," Associated Press News, May 4, 2017, www.apnews.com/4f0f4b38c0374d46bdcb2184065cd0c4.

17. For current numbers of civilian victims of the Syrian revolution, see Megan Price, Jeff Klingner, Anas Qtiesh, and Patrick Ball, "Full Updated Statistical Analysis of Documentation of Killings in the Syrian Arab Republic," Human Rights Data Analysis Group, commissioned by United Nations Office of the High Commissioner for Human Rights, June 13, 2013. See also Megan Price and Patrick Ball, "Full Updated Statistical Analysis of Documentation of Killings in the Syrian Arab Republic," Human Rights Data Analysis Group, May 2016.

18. See Human Rights Watch, *Death from the Skies; Deliberate and Indiscriminate Airstrikes on Civilians* (New York: Human Rights Watch, 2012), http://www.hrw.org/reports/2013/04/10/death-skies.

19. Zeid Ra'ad Al Hussein, International, Impartial and Independent Mechanism on International Crimes Committed in the Syrian Arab Republic, OHCHR, 2019, www.ohchr.org/EN/NewsEvents/Pages/DisplayNews.aspx?NewsID=21241.

Chapter Two

Demographic Engineering in Syria

Radwan Ziadeh

The 2011–2019 War in Syria has radically changed the demography of the country. Suggesting the possibility of the return of the previous demographic status to the prewar phase has become near to impossible; the Syrian population has gone down from 21,124,000—as per the official statistics issued by the Central Bureau of Statistics (CBS)[1]—to 18,284,000—as per the statistics of the populations shifts based on data issued by the United Nations and the World Bank.[2] The United Nations, according to the UN High Commissioner for Refugees (UNHCR), indicates that there are more than 3,300,000 refugees registered within its records.[3]

During the last seven years, the civil war[4] in Syria has turned into a regional one[5] that is fed on the conflict of regional and international interests and disguised by relying on the ability of the involved regional parties to have a dialogue and to come to common grounds in either Geneva, Astana, or elsewhere, where talks have been held to end the war. However, these talks have failed to put an end to the constant flow of refugees as well as to the victims' bleeding that never ceased, as the death toll went up to 400,000,[6] which is higher than the death toll for civil wars in Africa or in Latin America. The only comparable death toll is for the civil war in Cambodia,[7] where The Khmer Rouge regime killed over one million, and for the genocide in Rwanda, with a total number of more than 800,000 deaths.[8]

Today, we may argue that such demographic shifts are the outcome of a set of factors ignited by totality politics, which led to the displacement of such an immeasurable number of refugees compared to the numbers resulting from the previous civil wars in Africa or in Latin America. These factors can be concluded as follows:

FIRST: EXCESSIVE AIR FORCE EMPLOYMENT

First was the systematic, widespread, indiscriminate and excessive employment of the air force during the Syrian war in a way that made the war a remarkable one due to the number of its victims. The Syrian regime used the air force against civilians for the first time in July 2012[9] and never ceased to use it ever since. History has never witnessed such employment of an air force during civil wars except in particular cases (e.g., the civil war in Afghanistan that broke out back in March 1979 as a response to a local uprising carried out by the Mojahedin-e Khalq Army, the army affiliated with the People's Democratic Party of Afghanistan [PDPA]). The leaders of this war were two Afghani Presidents: Muhammad Taraki and Hafizullah Amin, who bombarded the city of Herat, the third largest city in the country, causing a death toll of approximately 5,000 to 25,000.[10]

The second case that history recalls of such nature is the civil war in Somalia, where Somali air force planes heavily raided the cities populated by the main clans of Isaac back in 1988. The raids targeted civilians of such clans during its military campaign against the Somali National Movement in the North. Civilians were also followed and attacked by Somali air force planes during their attempts to escape bombardment. The air force bombardment, along with the artillery shelling, left 50,000 to 250,000 civilians killed in addition to the total demolition of Somalia's second and third largest cities.[11]

The third case that history recalls of such nature is the war in Chechnya, where the Russian air force heavily bombarded the Chechen capital city of Grozny while mostly using indiscriminate and free-fall ammunition (including fuel-operated ammunition) in addition to employing massive artillery shells (in 1994–1995, 1996, and 1999–2000), leaving thousands dead. Some reports stated that during the siege of 1994–1995 alone[12] around 27,000 civilians were killed.

However, the number of victims that fell under the Syrian air force is deemed to be the largest of all the world's civil wars, as such raids targeted most of the cities and the villages that rebelled against the governmental army. As per Human Rights Watch,

> the Syrian regime air force has carried out a group of air strikes to support its targets via striking civilian areas including houses, medical centers, water supply stations, bakeries, crops and livestock.Such strikes are known for the main role played by the exploding barrels (barrel bombs) that are thrown down from the skies. In addition, sieges are supported in order to restrain the resistance movement within the areas that went out of the government's control.[13]

The Syrian air force has been known for dropping "barrel bombs," which are movable containers (oil or gas cylinders) that are dropped from a plane and filled with explosives or incendiary materials that are additively contained to increase the amount of explosion."[14] The amount of explosives that can be jammed into such barrels can severely destroy the targeted area due to the force of the explosion and the distance the barrels are dropped from. The Syrian army has dropped such barrels in noncombatant areas and killed thousands of civilians.[15] A report issued by Amnesty International stated that during the period of January 2014 to May 2015, only 1 percent of those who were killed by the barrel bombs were rebels.[16] Thus, such statistics prove the excessive employment of such weapons aimed at minimally targeting civilians and maximally displacing them. Hence, by the end of 2017, more than 97 percent of deaths involved civilians killed by barrel bombs, with children[17] making up 25 percent of the total.

A registered study conducted by five medical researchers, and based on the data provided by the Violation Documentation Center, argues that 143,630 deaths resulted from the dispute in Syria during the period from March 18, 2011, to December 31, 2016. It has also argued that Syrian civilians have made up 101,453 (70.6 percent) of such deaths, while the opposition- fighters made up 42,177 (29.4 percent). The deaths directly resulted from the widespread employment of weapons used by the air force, which resulted in 58,990 (57.3 percent) civilian deaths, including 8,285 females (74.6 percent), 13,810 children (79.4 percent), and almost 4,058 victims of opposition fighters (9.6 percent). The death toll for children increased from 8 to 9 percent (388 of 11,444). In 2016, the barrel bomb deaths alone reached 7,566, including 7,351 civilians (97.2 percent) and 2,007 children[18] (27.3 percent).

The report found that air force strikes were the main reason for such direct deaths of women and children. It also reached the conclusion that such strikes had disproportionate lethal effects on civilians, as increasing reliance on air strikes carried out by the Syrian government as well as by international partners have contributed to the results, indicating that children were killed due to such air bombardment. The report concluded that, in addition to one quarter of the deaths of 2016, the deaths resulting from the barrel bombs were mainly of civilians rather that opposition fighters, which indicates that the use of the barrel bombs violates international humanitarian law (IHL) and constitutes a war crime.[19]

Despite all these authenticated reports and during all his interviews, Bashar al-Assad kept denying the employment of barrel bombs. Moreover, during his BBC interview on February 10, 2015, he denied it by stating:

"We don't have barrel bombs.. We don't have barrels. I haven't heard of the army using barrels, or maybe, cooking pots,"[20] he said sarcastically.[21]

Moreover, when the Security Council Resolution 2139/2014[22] was unanimously adopted (i.e., including Russia and China, which were known for their vetoes against any resolution condemning the Assad regime), the resolution for the first time used the term "barrel bombs" as it called on all parties to immediately cease all attacks against civilians, as well as the indiscriminate employment of weapons in populated areas, including shelling and aerial bombardment, such as the employment of barrel bombs, and methods of warfare which are of a nature to cause superfluous injury or unnecessary suffering, and recalled in this regard the obligation to respect and ensure respect for international humanitarian law in all circumstances, and further recalled, in particular, the obligation to distinguish between civilian populations and fighters, and the prohibition against indiscriminate attacks, and attacks against civilians and civilian objects as such.[23] However, the Syrian regime challenged the UN and returned to its employment of such barrels few days following the issuance of the UN resolution in Aleppo as well as other areas falling under opposition control.[24]

Furthermore, areas like Darayya, which is almost seven kilometers away from Damascus and had a population of 250,000 before 2011, is reported to have been showered by more than 4,000[25] barrels. Actually, the Assistant Secretary-General of the United Nations, Stephen O'Brien, described the four-year besieged city as the "capital city of barrel bombs."[26]

Such systematic, widespread, indiscriminate, and excessive bombardment has played a vital role in the displacement of Syrian refugees. Moreover, in one of its reports, Human Rights Watch stated that the direct reason for people seeking refuge is related to the barrel bombs. Therefore, in order to stop the flow of refugees, these showers of barrel bombs must be ceased.[27]

SECOND: SIEGE

The United Nations Office for the Coordination of Humanitarian Affairs (OCHA) defines "siege" as the case when an area is surrounded by armed and acting forces and the consequent impact is that humanitarian assistance cannot be provided regularly and that the elderly, the sick, and the wounded cannot get out of such area regularly.[28]

However, siege was employed during the Syrian war as a weapon and the Independent International Commission of Inquiry on the Syrian Arab Republic has stated that the siege in Syria was

> carried out systematically and recklessly forcing the population to either collectively surrender or to starve to death. Such deprivation of food, water, power and medical care has led to malnutrition and deaths of the weak-health categories such as the elderly, toddlers, children and chronic cases. The besieged local communities, which were trapped between their inability to re-

ceive life essential materials and constant fear of death due to assassinations or bombardments, were exposed to severe psychological trauma and extreme despair.[29]

In addition, the civilian residents of the besieged areas around the country were exposed to restrictions, restraints, indiscriminate bombardment, and starvation. They were not allowed to leave their cities and were periodically deprived of medical evacuation. They were deprived of receiving vital food, health, and other essential supplies in an attempt to force those "in control" of such besieged areas to surrender. The sieging operations were mostly carried out by the Syrian regime along with its allied forces; however, such operations were also carried out by the armed opposing parties and the terrorist groups. Sieging operations were known for the common occurrence of war crimes all over Syria as such technique remained as the main method of war employed by all parties to the dispute. Such technique was recurrent as its penalty was never imposed or fulfilled, in a palpable violation of the international law of human rights and of the International Humanitarian Law.[30]

Sieging operations were first employed as a collective punitive mechanism of suppression at the very first stages of the Syrian war; a few days following the peaceful protests in the city of Daraa that broke out on March 18, 2011, the Syrian army started sieging the city on April 25 for a period of eleven days as the army started its "Operation Daraa"—as it referred to it—by "surrounding the city and by cutting water, power and communication off its residents."[31] As a first, the Syrian regime brought tanks, armored vehicles and helicopters to guarantee the imposing of the siege with the participation of more than 6,000 soldiers.[32] Up to 244 people were killed, mostly children.[33] However, in late 2012 the siege turned out to be a strategy followed by the government as per the slogan carved on walls by the state's army soldiers "Starve or Surrender," in order to impose a long-term siege. Such strategy was completely applied back 2013 in and has been regularly employed all over the country ever since as a means of collective punishment.[34]

The armed opposition has responded to such acts while employing the same means of war via sieging the pro-regime cities and villages, where civilians used to volunteer and join the *Shabiha* forces or the national defense forces; the state-sponsored militias of the Syrian government laid siege to Al-Fu'ah and Kafriya. Daesh has also developed sieging tactics during its siege of Deir-al-Zour.

However, we must differentiate between three levels of sieging with respect to legal and criminal liability, as such method as well as its impact on the social and the demographic shift should not be neglected by turning it into a part of "general practices" committed during the Syrian war.

The Syrian American Medical Society (SAMS),discussed the three levels of siege in its report "Slow Death,"[35] and these levels were later adopted by the Siege Watch Organization, which issued periodic reports for a period of four years (2015–2018) while watching the besieged[36] Syrian areas. These three levels were specified as follows:

Level 1: The highest level of siege, where limited amounts of supplies are smuggled or bribed into the besieged areas. In addition, the UN can negotiate to bring in limited medical and food shipments; however, residents of such besieged areas are perilously exposed to malnutrition, drought, and a lack of medical care. Besides, the area may be recurrently attacked by the sieging forces.

Level 2: A moderate level of sieging, where small amounts of supplies can be smuggled, bribed, or bought through black markets with extremely high prices. Delivery vehicles are not allowed to enter the besieged area; however, residents are able to reach alternative supplies such as local agriculture. In addition, the UN is able to negotiate to pass in small amounts of supplies and aid; however, such supplies are not sufficient for all residents. Hence, residents of such areas are exposed to malnutrition, drought, and the increasing risks of a lack of medical care. Besides, such areas are recurrently attacked by the sieging forces.

Level 3: The minimum level of sieging, where supplies are smuggled regularly and residents have regular outlets to reach alternative food resources such as local agriculture. In addition, the UN is able to negotiate to deliver some supplies; however, such supplies are not sufficient for all residents. Hence, residents of such areas are exposed to minor levels of malnutrition and drought and a mild risk of lack of medical care. Besides, such areas are attacked by the sieging forces, yet irregularly.[37]

In light of such systematic classification, we can compare the besieged areas and tackle such sieges as well as their outcomes to deliberate the strategies applied by the sieging authority whether it is the Syrian regime, the armed opposition, or Daesh.

As per the Security Council unanimously adopting Resolution 2268, which was issued on February 26, 2016, thirty cities and villages were marked as besieged areas and all parties involved were ordered to "provide prompt humanitarian aid all over the country comprehensively, continually and without facing any obstructions."[38]

Up untill the issuance of the resolution, the Syrian government along with its allies constituted the major sieging forces against the Syrian civilians. The reports issued by Siege Watch state that there are approximately fifty areas that can be described as besieged; however, there are only two areas—as per the resolution issued by the United Nations Security Council (UNSC)—that are described as besieged. These areas are Al-Fu'ah and Kafriya, located in the governorate of Idlib, which were sieged by the armed opposing groups, and the area of Deir-al-Zour, which was sieged by both Daesh and the Syrian government.[39]

Moreover, most of the areas that were sieged by the Syrian regime—if not all areas—were classified as Level 1, which is the severest of all levels, while the ones sieged by the armed opposition such as Al-Fu'ah and Kafriya were classified as Level 3. This mere comparison indicates the difference between the systematic and strategic siege implemented by the regime to achieve certain political, military, and (probably) demographic goals and the one implemented by the opposition that aimed at exchanging military acts and punishing the counterparty. Eventually, the Syrian civilians submitted to such acts and were the victims of starvation and sieging policy for several years.

Ever since 2013, when the government started to employ sieges systematically against opposition areas it lost control of, and the siege policy was adopted and implemented as a widespread strategy that took over all the Syrian governorates, which went out of control, most of these areas became completely isolated from the outer world.[40] This strategy has left behind a man-made drastic catastrophe along with more than one million victims.[41]

Despite all the resolutions issued by the United Nations Security Council to break the siege of such areas and to allow humanitarian aid into them, the Syrian regime turned a deaf ear to such resolutions in the best-case scenarios and sought military escalation in the worst-case ones. Despite the issuance of the Security Council's unanimously adopted Resolution 2401 in February 2018, via which a demand was made to break the siege imposed over the populated areas including Eastern Ghouta, to cease the deprivation of food and essential medications, as well as to permit relief and aid organizations to provide "a prompt, safe and unhindered evacuation of all civilians willing to leave such areas" and to cease fire all over Syria,[42] the Syrian regime's response was shown a day later, when chlorine gas was used in Ghouta, leaving more than 23 dead.[43] Moreover, Russia, as per the statements made by the Russian Minster of Foreign Affairs, Lavrov, declared that the ceasefire did not include the terrorist groups based in Ghouta. This was an attempt to justify Russia's ongoing military operations there. Lavrov also added that the truce would cover only few hours of the day and asked the civilians to leave Ghouta,[44] repeating the same scenario pulled out in Aleppo.

Furthermore, the Amnesty International, in its report "Left to Die under Siege,"[45] has described life in Eastern Ghouta and referred to the existence of solid proof of the war crimes committed by the Syrian government during its siege of Ghouta. The report describes the illegal killings of Ghouta's be-sieged civilians as well as the Syrian government's siege of the area that was carried out systematically in a way that merits the siege be labled a war crime. In addition, the report casts light on the agonizing struggle that more than 163,000 civilians had to go through to survive while living under siege in Eastern Ghouta.[46]

The report states that "the lives of the people of Ghouta were ruined through blood shedding; as they were trapped and lived under siege and fire on all fronts without having the slightest chance to escape air strikes as well as the illegal bombardment carried out by the governmental forces. Moreover, such suffering was doubled by the shortage of food, clean water and essential supplies (i.e., life for this population was miserable and tiresome).[47] In addition to the daily bombardment, life in Ghouta kept going from bad to worse, as supplies of food, clean water, medical care, and essential materials including power and fuel were extremely limited and checkpoints were controlled by either the governmental forces, or the armed groups that limited civilian movement inside and outside Eastern Ghouta. In addition, the governmental forces denied access to the agencies of the UN as well as other humanitarian and relief organizations to the area.

More than 200 persons died from starvation or lack of adequate medical care during the period extending from October 21, 2012, to January 31, 2015, as per the statistics of the Syrian American Medical Society (SAMS).[48]

The emergence of the black market (war economy) has enabled smugglers and militant groups or government officials to make fortunes at the expense of the civilians; as the Syrian governmental forces were confiscating food supplies periodically at checkpoints, residents were forced to purchase goods from the black market, paying ten times as much for what they can get in downtown Damascus.

Therefore, all areas that were besieged for long terms during the period extending from 2013 to 2017 or 2018 were exposed to either forced displacement, cities exchange, local reconciliation, or evacuation agreements, as defined by both the Syrian regime and Russia. This reveals the fact that siege as a strategy has greatly succeeded in destroying local resistance movements of the besieged communities and forced such communities to "surrender"[49] lest more victims fall down daily due to either siege and food shortage or due to indiscriminate aerial bombardments, barrel bombs, or the excessive employment of chlorine gas attacks.

If we go back to the quantitative comparison of the besieged areas and the incrementally worse condition of such areas due to the government's growing awareness of their vital role in taking down the resistance movements via imposing sieging as a collective punitive mechanism, and the reduction of the population of such areas compared to their status before the siege, we can conclude that this strategy was a success as it managed to achieve a strategic recipe for establishing a new demography in Syrian society. Assad has personally denied intending for such displacement movements to constitute a demographic shift[50] in Syria, following his visit to Darayya;[51] however, the reduction of the population of besieged areas indicates that the Syrian regime has discovered the efficiency of sieging in achieving the aspired for demographic shift.

With the emergence of the first phases of such human catastrophe back in 2012, the UN Office for the Coordination of Humanitarian Affairs started to file its periodic reports regarding the human situation in Syria; however, there was no reference to any data on any besieged areas in the country.[52] It was clear that the UN did not take the Homs siege into consideration despite the fact that on June 9, 2012, the Syrian regime forces shut down the last and only passage between the besieged areas in the old suburbs of Homs: Alkhalediah, Albaiada, Jub Aljundli, Alqusour, and Alqurabis Ghouta. This made whole areas fall under full siege[53] for two years. Such partial siege turned into a full one via spreading tanks and vehicles in Homs preventing the delivery of any food supplies to the rebelling areas except for those smuggled in. Besides, services to these areas were cut off and their residents were forced to leave as 5,000 of their sons were killed during the first months of the revolution. Moreover, following the shutting of the last passage, whoever was spotted near the area was either detained or assassinated. Getting near the area has become next to impossible.[54]

Later, the first Security Council Resolution 2139/2014[55] was issued as the Council expressed its deep concerns regarding the rapidly deteriorating human situation in Syria, especially when it came to the devastating status of hundreds of civilians trapped in the besieged areas, most of whom were trapped by the Syrian armed forces while the remaining civilians were besieged by the opposing groups. This is in addition to the devastating status of more than three million civilians living in hard-to-reach areas.[56] The Council has also expressed its sorrow for the obstacles facing the delivery of humanitarian aid and assistance to all Syrian civilians in need as well as for its failure to deliver such aid. The resolution has also called on "all parties to promptly break the siege over the populated areas including: the areas located in the old suburbs of Homs, Nabel and Zahraa (in Aleppo), Muadamiyat al-Sham (in Rif Dimashq), Yarmok (in Damascus), Eastern Ghouta (in Rif Dimashq), and Darayya (in Rif Dimashq) in addition to other locations. It has demanded all parties permit deliverance of humanitarian aid including medical care and demanded such parties cease deprivation of food supplies and medications indispensable for civilians' survival. The resolution has also demanded that all parties allow safe, prompt, and unhindered evacuation for those willing to leave such areas. It also emphasized the necessity for all parties involved to come to mutual ground regarding holding truces for human purposes and to cease fire for local truces to allow humanitarian organizations to reach all the damaged areas. The resolution has also recalled that starving civilians as a means of war is prohibited as per the International Humanitarian Law.[57]

Throughout its report, the Independent International Commission of Inquiry on the Syrian Arab Republic—formed by the Office of the High Commissioner for Human Rights (OHCHR)—has fruitfully summarized the impact of the siege and its relation to the demographic shift in Syria, stating that "all aspects that cannot be tolerated in life or death under a siege have increased due to the employment of prohibited chemical weapons and cluster munitions within heavily populated areas that are packed with civilians while aiming at threatening them and spreading despair amongst their lines. Eventually, civilians are left with no other choice but to leave their houses and get internally displaced. Mostly, they are displaced into certain specified destinations that they did not choose; however, such destinations were specified as per the frame of the "evacuation agreements." The siege policy has led to the displacement of almost 50,000 Syrians, including: males, females, and children, in the light of the local truce agreements held in 2018. [58]

THIRD: SECTARIAN CRIMES OR CRIMES BASED ON GENDER

In all civil wars in which large-scale massacres have taken place on ethnic or sectarian levels, or those where widespread rape has been practiced, an intended demographic shift occurs. Sectarian or ethnic massacres as well as aim at spreading terror and fear amongst civilians, in this case those belonging to the opposing sect or ethnicity. A person belonging to this group is not immune to murder, defilement, or physical elimination simply because he or she belongs to a wholly different sect or ethnicity, which is in itself a sufficient justification for killing or "shaming" men through sexual abuse of their wives, daughters, or children.

These practices and direct relationships have been studied largely in civil wars in Africa, or the Balkan War, where ethnic or sectarian massacres and ethnic cleansing have occurred. [59] Salzmann states that there were more than 20,000 cases of sexual assault in the Balkans during the war period committed by all parties involved; however, the largest and the incomparable proportion was carried out by the Serbs against the Muslim women of Bosnia and Herzegovina as well as Catholic Croat women. In the past, rape was seen as a product of war; however, reports in the Balkan War show that this type of attack does not aim at "inhumanizing" the opponent alone, it is a "voluntary act" that aims at achieving future political objectives through ethnic cleansing and claiming ownership of the land by clearing it of the other, and thus the Serbian political and military commanders had been planning this type of crime in advance to support Bosnian Serbs to build a pure cultural, religious, linguistic, and ethnical Serbia. [60] This was reiterated by the Serbs during the Kosovo War that broke out in 1998, where rape and other forms of sexual violence were employed by all parties to the conflict and continued to be employed throughout the 1999 refugee crisis. Serbs used this tactic by a much higher proportion. Rape was not a rare and isolated act committed by both Serbian and Yugoslav forces, but was deliberately employed as a tool to terrorize the civilians, extort money from families, and drive people to flee their homes. Rape reinforced the goal of forcing Albanians (Kosovo residents belonging to the Albanian minority) to flee Kosovo.[61]

As for the civil wars in Africa, Turshen asserts that militias and regular armies employed rape in civil wars "systematically to strip women of their economic and political sovereignty, as women's assets are primarily in their productivity, labor and secondly in their possessions and their access to the value of assets such as land and livestock.[62] In a field study of the civil wars in Mozambique and Rwanda, it was concluded that systematic rape is a socially constructed experience, which is produced through a series of political decisions.[63] Turshen reaches the same conclusion that rape is essentially a political decision and not just one of the symptoms of the war. Rape has political goals to achieve and at the top of these goals is the collective fear that leads to emigration, exodus, or collective displacement of the enemy.[64]

The crimes based on sectarian and ethnic grounds may have been more prevalent in the Syrian war than rape, but may have brought about the very political goal of cleansing or "homogenization," according to the expression that Assad has repeatedly used, as conveyed by Jamil Hassan, the Chief of Military Intelligence: "The huge number of the wanted people will not make it difficult to complete the plan (which aims at arresting more than 3 million Syrians, both internally and externally, wanted by the Air Force Intelligence Directorate), because a Syria that has 10 million honest, obedient to leadership is definitely way better than Syria with 30 million vandals."[65]

This reveals that there is a political decision to eliminate this huge number of activists and political detainees by killing them under torture[66] or by physical elimination inside prisons in order to push the largest number of their families and relatives to flee due to arrest and then elimination.

It was clear that the regime's aims (especially the security bodies and the intelligence services, according to Khader Khdour) "were to ensure full loyalty of the people of Homs who are seen as a controlled institution dominated by coastal Alawites. Despite the fact that the Alawites of Homs are civilians, most of their family members or neighbors work for the army or in the intelligence services, which contributed early to the early "militarization" of the Alawite community,[67] which explains the very high percentage of volunteers from Homs-Alawites in early stages, especially from the area of Zahra[68] in the so-called "*Shabiha*," which the regime calls the "national defense." These militias represent a paramilitary force with an organizational structure, tactics, training, subculture, and function (often similar to that of a professional army), but it is not included as part of the official armed forces of the state.[69] Specifically, these militias commit the most horrifying and brutal sectarian massacres, such as the massacres of Karam Al-Zaitoun and Houla, both of which took place back in 2012 and played a major role in the demographic displacement and change of social features of the city of Homs.

What matters is that we follow the sequence of massacres committed on a sectarian basis while relying on three main criteria:

First: To determine the extent of the number of victims belonging to a particular sect during the war period in Syria.

Second: It relates to the first exclusively, and may not be separated. Using sectarian slogans (signs—clothing—symbols and others that are used to glorify the particular sect and sanctify its victims) before, during, and after the massacre.

Third: Identification of the perpetrators of the massacre and whether they belonged to a different sect from the victims' sect during the massacre.[70]

In light of these three criteria, a number of massacres committed during the Syrian revolution can be identified as committed by either by the regime or by armed factions, namely Jabhat al-Nusra or ISIS.

This report will provide a detailed analysis of these massacres in the order of their occurrence and the role they had specifically in relation to the displacement and demographic shift in Syria, according to the three criteria that will determine what a sectarian massacre is, as well as the direct relationship between these sectarian massacres and the waves of displacement or migration, demonstrating the motive behind the perpetration of such massacres in these areas.

This is what we will try to prove about Homs. This can be generalized to other areas, where sectarian massacres have taken place at the sectarian "cross-lines" in Homs (twenty-two massacres), Hama (eight massacres), Rif Dimashq (five massacres), and Tartous (two massacres), according to the Syrian Network for Human Rights.[71]

With the rise of peaceful protests in Homs, the largest numbers reached more than 10,000 participants in the so-called big sit-in in the square on April 18, 2011.[72] The Syrian security services quickly mobilized Alawite men to respond to the anti-government protests, sending them in counterprotests to Sunni neighborhoods encouraging sectarian discourse. The Al-Zahra area, the largest Alawite gathering in Homs, became the focus of the pro-government "*Shabiha*" militias.[73] That initially drove security forces' vehicles to the neighborhoods where the protests were held to open fire[74] on protesters. Then a majority of snipers, who spread across all the high buildings in different areas of Homs.

In response, the so-called "security of protests" arose as the number of Syrian army defectors increased after they refused to shoot protesters. With the increase in the number of people killed as a result of peaceful protests, the number of armed men within these protests increased in order to protect them and to return the fire. At the beginning of 2012, the number of militants increased significantly in the Bab Amr area in Homs, and they established weapons training camps.[75] They subsequently liberated a number of checkpoints, and at the beginning of February 2012, the regime began preparing for a large-scale military campaign to invade and control the neighborhood. For the first time, the regime used heavy military vehicles in the attack, especially T-72 tanks, as well as reconnaissance aircraft.[76] In the end, after 28 days of resistance, the regime succeeded in breaking into the neighborhood and the fighters withdrew to the southern countryside in order to reduce the number of civilian casualties.[77] Then it can be said that the Syrian Revolution entered into a whole new phase with regard to armaments, and at the same time the regime realized that it would not be able to kill peaceful protestors as easily as it did over the previous 11 months and it would face a new kind of armed resistance. The regime therefore developed its principle with regard to ignoring international criticism, no matter how severe it might be, focusing on the principle of absolute military power and, more importantly, ensuring full loyalty within the army units or security patrols sent by military or air force intelligence. This principle of loyalty has been defined by belonging to the "Alawite sect" and the conflict in Homs has been altered totally by the question of why things have evolved so sharply into militarization and who is responsible for employing heavy weapon to suppress a group of peaceful protesters. It has become a military conflict between the "Sunnis," who form the opposition, and the "Alawites," who defend the government narrative and form the backbone of the security bodies and must "stand in solidarity" with each other to the limit to defend their "power," "state," and "presence."

Then we find a recurring pattern: A sectarian massacre is committed by *Shabiha* in the cross-lines in Homs followed by a wave of mass displacement from the same area due to evacuation. The first major sectarian massacres took place in Homs in the Karam Al-Zaitoun on March 9–11, 2012, preceded by several sectarian incidents in which gunmen targeted displaced civilians in Al-Zahraa, an Alawite neighborhood, on January 26, 2012, killing four people. Armed pro-government *Shabiha* militants responded by killing fourteen people, including eight children from the Bhadur family in the Karam al-Zaitoun neighborhood.[78] After the army ended military operations in the neighborhood, the militias, most of them from the "Hallool" family, who live in the Alawite neighborhood of Akrama, killed 47 people, the majority of whom were children and women, and mutilated their bodies. The mutilation of dead bodies and the employment of blunt instruments reflects a criminal dimension against a sectarian background. Although witnesses form the neighborhood knew the names of those, who committed the massacre, the government refused even to summon them or bring them in for investigation.[79] These "sectarian massacres" were pursued in "Sunni" neighborhoods of Homs, and the al-Rifai neighborhood witnessed a similar massacre on

March 12, 2012, in which 39 corpses had mutilated faces and bodies.[80] Human Rights Watch quoted a description from a witness of the massacre as follows: "When I arrived at Bab al-Drib, there were sixteen bodies, all belonging to women and children. Some children were struck in the head with blunt instruments, and you could see the brain outside the skull. Some of them have traces of gunshot wounds to the head and sensitive areas. Some women are naked, almost completely."[81]

On the same date, the *Shabiha* collected Sunni families from the Adawiya region, including a large number of women and children, and slaughtered them with knives.[82] The massacre was described by Human Rights Watch as follows: "They entered Karam al-Zaitoun, Al-Adawiya and Al-Rifai neighborhoods on March 11. One eyewitness said that the residents, who escaped the Al-Adaweya neighborhood, told him that *Shabiha* had entered the area at around 3 pm. Residents told him that some women were raped and some families were killed in their homes. He said that Free Syrian Army personnel were able to enter some houses on the outskirts of the Karam al-Zaitoun and extracted 47 bodies from six separate families. They found the bodies in five houses."[83]

These massacres were repeated almost in the same way in Deir Baalbah in April 2012 and in the Al-Shamas neighborhood in May 2012, concluding with the Houla massacre on May 25, 2012, in which more than 107 people were killed.[84] The Independent International Commission of Inquiry on the Syrian Arab Republic, which opened a special investigation into the massacre on the basis of a resolution of the United Nations Human Rights Council in Geneva, stated the following:

> The evidence gathered by the Commission of Inquiry indicates that, during a 24–hour period beginning on the afternoon of May 25, 2012, at least 100 people were killed in the town of Tel Taldo. Shortly after the Friday prayer, a protest took place near the city center. It appears that the government security forces opened fire on the protestors or bombed them.[85] Then the shelling continued by government forces all day, the Commission of Inquiry was able to verify damage caused by shelling of the buildings by comparing satellite imagery on the morning of May 25 and the morning of May 26. Much of the damage appeared to have been caused by mortar shells, including large-caliber mortar shells, heavy machine guns or light artillery. . . . Most of the victims were women and children, most of whom appear to have been killed while in their homes. The evidence indicates that they were shot dead at close range on the upper part of the body. The killings took place in at least two locations.

The report described what can be seen as the signs or evidence of a sectarian massacre. The report described testimonies collected from people who told the Commission of Inquiry that they were among the first to arrive at the scene. These witnesses described the use of sharp tools to kill Abdul Razzaq's family. Many interviewees described the stab wounds and the apparent use of machetes and the like. Another person claimed that he found many knives, and that he found one of them with the inscription "We Sacrifice ourselves for Hussein"—which is the slogan of Shiites. The Commission saw a videotape of a knife with a pattern like this.[86]

In fact, it is possible to count more than nine sectarian massacres that took place in Homs alone throughout the period extending from February 2012 to June 2012. More than 593 civilians[87] were killed in these massacres, according to the Syrian Network for Human Rights. But the sectarian massacres do not really aim at killing the largest number of the other sect, but at "terrorizing" and intimidating them in order to encourage them to flee and emigrate. What matters here is the "brutality" of the crime and its horror, being swamped in the "impossible to imagine" and the absence of a legal, moral, or humanitarian justification for its perpetration. It is a collective punitive act carried out against the other sect.

The perpetuation of these horrific sectarian massacres was accompanied by the practice of rape, but not by the same prevalence; however, rape remained a common practice within the Assad regime's secret detention camps and within the security bodies as a way to humiliate detainees and to exercise maximum psychological harm to their families, especially if these detainees were taken hostage to force their husbands, children, or siblings to surrender. So, harassment, sexual assault, and rapes have become more common in Syrian jails as part of repressive practices. Unfortunately, sexual violence committed by pro-regime forces has been only slightly documented for a number of reasons, because few survivors dare to speak, and reporting sexual violence is a very sensitive issue to tackle within Syrian conservative society and carries risks for the victim. The honor of the family is closely linked to women as sexual abuse of women brings shame to all family members.[88]

Therefore, many former detainees, whether or not they are raped, refuse to say so and prefer to live in a long-term psychological conflict or with a stigma of fear of retaliation or expression of what happened to them.

The report conveys that

> rape is practiced as a powerful tool to terrorize people. Rumors quickly spread early in the revolution that women in detention would be at risk of being sexually abused. This has deterred activists from playing an increasing role in the opposition. The Syrian government has also sought through the practice of rape to increase antagonism between different sects, not only to mobilize and consolidate support from minorities, but also to frame the conflict as a battle between Alawites and Sunnis rather than a struggle for democracy. The prevalence of sexual violence was targeted at those belonging to the Sunni community.[89]

FOURTH: DISPLACEMENT AND FORCED DISPLACEMENT

Wars are always accompanied by internal displacement, which is defined by the UN principles as people or groups of people that had to or were forced to flee or leave their homes or usual habitations, especially due to or in order to avoid the results of armed conflicts, general violence, human rights violations, or catastrophes, both of manmade and natural causes, and who did not cross the borders of an internationally recognized state.[90] Therefore, the internally displaced people are similar to refugees, as they share the same situation; however, they differ in that they do not cross a border to a state other than that, where the war took place.

Thus, it is not very peculiar that the number of Syrian displaced persons is increasing due to the aggravation of violence and conflict in Syria. Yet, we are concerned with the study of the relation between displacement and demographic shifts, (e.g., how displacement became one of the factors leading to demographic shift in Syria during the years of war). Such relation stems from following certain policies and bills issued by the Syrian government to turn such a temporary displacement due to war into a permanent one, thus eventually leading into the shift in demography of different Syrian cities and governorates.

Displacement does not necessarily lead to a demographic shift, if there were clear policies with guarantees that the displaced population shall return to their home regions after the war or violence ends, in which the UN foundations should take part as per the Pinheiro Principles,[91] which set the international criteria in terms of the displaced and refugees returning to their homes. They clearly state that

> those who were displaced by the forces beyond their control and power must not face the possibility of losing their homes, lands or properties just because they were forced, one way or another, to leave them in pursuit of safety and protection. Therefore, even if such return is not possible or safe by the displaced persons themselves, for example, when they chose to seek asylum or refugee resettlement in another safe country and even if they do not have actual intent to return, yet all their properties must be kept such as refugees and displaced people's lands and properties.

So, for millions of refugees and displaced people, who do not wish to return to their original home, both the relevant authorities and international entities should work hard to preserve rights and private property.[92]

The principles continue: "return does not include only returning to the original home country, but also returning to the original house." These basic principles and standards are based mainly on international law, including a countless number of resolutions of the Security Council and the General Assembly of the United Nations over the past sixty years that expressly tackled the right of property reinstitution. Both the international and national human rights institutions have asserted the right of all the refugees and internally displaced people to return freely to their homes and to recover their houses and properties, which they were denied, or to receive proper compensation for the unrecoverable properties. These principles are now considered basic elements for any constructive peace strategy.[93]

Opposing these principles, Assad's regime has issued a series of official laws, as well as both written and non-written directives, punishing all the population of rebelling areas and denying them the right to return to their villages, cities, and properties or rendering such return impossible or extremely difficult, due to the complete or partial destruction of properties and theft of entire homes, furniture, and contents and the burning of what was left. This is a phenomenon the pro-Assad call *"Ta'feesh,"* which means stealing everything from houses such as furniture, appliances, wires and even floor tiles, thus rendering reuse of such houses impossible in order to sell them, which actually took place in many of the cities recovered by the Syrian regime from opposition such as Darayya, Aleppo, Douma, Haresta, Al-Zabadany, and Madaya among others,[94] which led to displacement, thus causing non-return due to complete loss of properties even after the war or violence concluded in such areas. Therefore, some refer to such actions as strategy, for they were repeated in all the cities without exception and there was no single piece of news holding anyone responsible for such violations and actually brought to national courts or no lawsuits filed against any of them, despite the fact that there were thousands of videos showing the action of *Ta'feesh* undertaken[95] completely and openly, which refers to some sort of political support and approval of top leadership in order to reward the regime's soldiers or *"Shabeeha"*[96] for their efforts, aiming mainly at forcing people to move towards certain regions that were previously under the control of rebellions. Despite Assad's reinstitution of power over some cities, the return of people to such cities remained conditional, and even when they returned it was totally shocking to find that all of their property and belongings were destroyed. This rendered their return impossible, for they lacked the money required to restore their inhabitable homes.[97] Such a strategy has a very obvious objective: to ensure complete control over these areas through forcing people to have security permission before returning to their homes. Often, negotiations to remove people take place after long sieges by the regime's forces and their allies, which include putting certain areas under siege, cutting power and water supplies as well as human aid including food and medical supplies, and random bombing by mortar and barrel bombs before asking for surrender. Then people shall have only one choice (that is, displacement), which is forced relocation against the civilians' will. Many residents' agreements were conducted between 2017 and 2018.

FORCED DISPLACEMENT AGREEMENTS

Until the beginning of 2018, the Syrian regime managed in collaboration with both Russians and Iranians to force rebellions to clear their areas in return for moving North, namely Idlib. These agreements were referred to by both the Syrian regime and the Russians as "reconciliation agreements," but for the rebellions these were forced displacement agreements to force civilian residents to leave their homes and cities in return for their lives in case they decided to stay in Idlib. The number of areas witnessing displacement in Syria increased to more than 30 cities and towns.

FORCED DISPLACEMENT IN HOMS

The first forced displacement took place in 2014, February 2014 to be exact, as around 3,000 civilians and militants were driven out of Homs to the areas falling under the control of the Syrian opposition up North. This was the first and last displacement operation to be undertaken under the supervision of the UN.[98]

A series of multiparty negotiations began to be held between the opposition and the government with the mediation of Russia and Iran and the supervision of the UN. These negotiations led to an agreement to move the remaining civilians and militants outside Homs. During February 7–9, 2014, the evacuation of downtown areas under siege began through a series of forced displacement operations. The UN Human Settlements Program report issued in June 2014 stated that only 100 people were not evacuated.[99] Although these were called evacuation operations, the agreements were actually some kind of forced surrender in which the residents under siege had no other choice but to surrender or die.[100]

In the presence of UN observers, both civilians and militants were mobilized in green governmental buses, and were moved to the Al-Waer neighborborood or the northern countryside outside Homs. These buses later became a symbol of forced displacement all over Syrian cities.

AL-WAER NEIGHBORHOOD

Governmental siege in Homs started in October 2013 when the armed opposing militants in Homs were fighting the governmental forces and the vast majority of the Al-Waer neighborhood's population, estimated to be 70,000 to 100,000, had its movement restricted. They were also unable to get food, medicine, and fuel. Even students and government employees, who were given permission to exit and enter the neighborhood, often faced harassment at the checkpoints, as well as, detention in some cases. The siege was increased gradually, especially in 2016, when bread was totally prohibited, which led the besieged residents to grind cereals they used to receive in aid to make bread. Eventually, Al-Waer residents relied completely on aid shipments that arrived irregularly and did not cover their needs.[101]

Amnesty International examined some video recordings from open sources showing the attacks that took place during the last year of the siege and found out that the recordings actually confirmed the statements of eyewitnesses regarding air strikes in highly populated areas and the destruction of the residential areas, as well as the impact of such strikes on civilians, especially children, who were burned due to the use of incendiary bombs. One last excessive attack that lasted over one month starting on February 7, 2017, made the residents surrender eventually.[102] A negotiation committee representing both civilians and militants of the Al-Waer neighborhood started talks with the government mid-2014, which led to a multistage agreement in December 2015 and a discontinuous truce in 2016. The agreement made in 2015 resulted in the evacuation of militants from Al-Waer. Yet the agreement failed by the end of 2016. In March 2017, an agreement sponsored by Russia put the area under the power of the government and led to the evacuation of 20,000 people in a scattered manner including all the remaining militants.[103]

The evacuation operation took place between March 18 and May 21 as twelve groups of displaced people were sent to three opposition sites. These were North of Aleppo governorate, North of Homs governorate, and Idlib governorate. Many of the displaced people were distributed to temporary camps that lacked necessities. The most inhumane circumstances are those of the Zoghra camp, northeast of Aleppo governorate, with over 7,500 refugees.[104]

The UN participation in the Homs agreement and forced displacement of people was controversial as the UN was severely criticized for its failure to protect those who were forced to leave under the agreement. The Syrian government arrested hundreds of them and interrogated them and the reports stated that some of them were tortured and killed.[105]

As a direct result of this scenario, the UNHCR issued the Minimum Standards for participation in humanitarian interagency evacuations informed by international humanitarian and international human rights law,[106] in order to guarantee that the UN agencies in the future would act according to such laws. Also, the Siege Watch report added that the document only included a few of the instructive principles of the process, stating the complex situation of Syria and that it failed to improve the forced movement and to make actual changes in the role played by the UN agencies in such operations, exactly as in Homs two years ago.[107]

FORCED DISPLACEMENT IN ALEPPO

However, the largest displacement operation took place in Aleppo, as the city witnessed in the period between 2012 and 2016 massive actions between the Syrian government and the armed opposing militias for over four years, during which the city was split in two: into an eastern section under the control of armed opposing militias and a western section controlled by the government. On July 7, 2016, the Syrian government started putting the eastern section of Aleppo under siege, including 250,000 to 275,000 people, most of whom were civilians, and where food, medicines, and supplies were restricted.[108]

The deterioration in human conditions and the massive bombing led the armed opposing groups to give in eventually and to negotiate with the government. Negotiations started in early December 2016 and were remotely held between representatives of both Russia and the Levant Liberals Islamic movement. On December 13 an agreement was reached between sides and it included evacuating all fighters of the armed groups north of Aleppo govern-orate. The agreement's terms did not include evacuating civilians, yet the vast majority of those who were in the area at the time, estimated as around 37,000 persons, chose to leave due to the horrible events they witnessed over the past months, in addition to the fact that they questioned the government's promises to guarantee their safety.[109] This shed the light on Assad's strategy of forced displacement committed against civilians' will.

Although the UN Security Council avoided using the term forced displacement and preferred the term evacuation under Russian pressure, resolution 2382 mentioned the claims to immediate break of siege of civilian areas and stated the fear of the deterioration of human conditions in Aleppo and that a large portion of Aleppo's population needed evacuation and humanitarian aid ASAP.[110]

It stated that all parties should stop depriving civilians of basic foods and medications and enable relief agencies to "perform speed and safe evacuation without any obstacles for all civilians who wish to leave." Yet the legal definition of what happened in Aleppo is forced displacement, which is a solid crime as per international law as "civilians were told that they should leave or risk being targeted by the armed forces; therefore, this is forced displacement." Additionally, force used in forced displacement is not physical force alone but also the threat to use force or the fear of violence or forcing.[111]

The Rome Statute of the International Criminal Court states that a crime against humanity includes "forced displacement or removal of residents" or "depriving of access to food and medicine thus resulting in destruction of part of the population."[112] The UN spent, according to Ben Taub, five months from July until December 2016 asking the Syrian government's permission to deliver food supplies and medical supplies to eastern Aleppo, yet the permission was never granted. Therefore, the people of Aleppo were starved and frozen. Yet the UN did not provide aid without the permission of Assad's regime according to the UN statute, as the regime's government is the government representing the Syrian State in the UN system."[113] When the regime refused to allow UN aid to enter Madaya by road as the death toll was rising, the UN threatened to deliver the aid by air. The regime did not yield and the UN never dropped a basket of food and the Syrians under siege remained under the mercy of the Syrian regime, which unfortunately did not have any mercy at all.[114]

Assad's assaults in eastern Aleppo were characterized as crimes of war and crimes against humanity and eventually the regime, with the support of Russia, forced the armed groups to evacuate eastern Aleppo and its surroundings, thus rendering Aleppo a wreck. Eastern Aleppo witnessed a genocide that affected the vast majority of its residents."[115] The regime's allies bombed eastern Aleppo for four years and reached their climax with the savage siege for a whole year, thus forcing the remaining armed groups to sign the evacuation agreement, as the governmental forces and the Russian forces described it. The evacuation agreement was also used in the Security Council resolution 2328 for Aleppo as eastern Aleppo underwent complete evacuation of its population, which was a first in the modern history of the Middle East.[116]

The last assault to break Aleppo was in late September 2016, as due to the Russian air forces superiority after Russian direct intervention in Syria in September 2015,[117] soon the governmental forces regained 15–20 percent of the part of city that was under the control of the opposition.[118]

On November 4, 2016, Russian president Putin declared a one-sided truce in Aleppo and declared four human passages for those who wished to leave eastern Aleppo. Although only a small number of civilians decided to exit through these passages, the civilians had a previous experiment with these passages that were declared through Bustan al-Qasr and Saladin, according to activists who spoke to Siege Watch at the time. Ttwo people tried to use the passages and were killed, and their dead bodies remain there because people couldn't evacuate them due to snipers.[119]

On November 27, 2016, the governmental forces, relying upon the Russian air forces, managed to take over the Hanano neighborhood in eastern Aleppo.[120] During efforts to split the eastern section into two, thousands started fleeing the section under opposition control. They were taken to a center in Jebrin and on the same day the armed opposition groups retreated towards the southern neighborhoods within the shrinking section to avoid falling into a trap. An agreement was reached with the People's Defense Units (YPG), by which the Kurds would enter the areas abounded by the opposition, thus creating a neutral frontier and allowing some of the population to stay in their homes. Nevertheless, the areas were surrendered to governmental forces, which eventually completely took over the northern regions of eastern Aleppo including Assakhour neighborhood, Askeikh Khedr, Hidaria, and Sliman Alhalaby. [121]

On December 5, 2016, a resolution was submitted by New Zealand, Spain, and Egypt to the UN Security Council for ceasing firing for seven days in eastern Aleppo, yet both Russia and China used their vetoes against it. On December 6, 2016, as an anti-proposal the armed groups in eastern Aleppo offered a three-point agreement calling for a human truce for five days, medical evacuation for 500 persons, and civilian evacuation toward the northern countryside of Aleppo, as well as launching negotiations between the activists concerned with Aleppo's future. Yet, the Syrian government turned all offers down under Russian pressure, and by December 7, 2016, the Syrian governmental troops, mainly confirmed from Lebanese militias such as Hezbollah, Iraqi militias, and the Islamic Revolutionary Guard Corps (IRGC), managed to take over about 75 percent of the region that used to be under opposition control. The next day the International Committee of the Red Cross and the Syrian Arabic Red Crescent took a very risky trip to Dar Al- Safaa in the old city to rescue 150 persons who had been trapped in actions, as they were taking refuge in what used to be an elderly retirement home that was extended to provide care for patients with mental health needs or physical impairments, as dozens of civilians were seeking protection there. [122]

The International Committee of the Red Cross estimated on December 23 that about 34,000 persons left eastern Aleppo and the evacuation was complete. The World Health Organization (WHO) stated that in total 811 patients were referred to hospitals in western Aleppo and Idlib, including 100 women and 150 children, and among those around 100 patients who needed special care were taken to hospitals in Turkey and the other patients were referred to 8 hospitals in western Aleppo's countryside and Idlib. Dr. David Naut, who treated some of those who were evacuated in Idlib, said "they seemed as if they were extracted from some arrest camp. They were not only injured but they also suffered from dehydration, malnutrition and mental shocks. [123] And those who were evacuated were distributed among the western Aleppo countryside, Jebrin and western Aleppo, which were still under the control of the Syrian government."

The United Nations reported that it had received information on 82 executions held in early December 2016. On January 20, 2017, the Office of the High Commissioner for Human Rights (OHCHR) confirmed that they had "further corroboration of executions and missing persons." A number of these deaths, which are believed to have been carried out by the government-allied militias, were reported in Kalasa: The Ajam family (five members), the Hassan family (five members), the El-Masry family (four members), and an unidentified family (eleven members). In Fardous, the Qasir family (six members) and the Hajjar family (twelve members) were reported as killed.[124]

Further killings were reported on December 25, 2016, in a series of field executions in Jabrin, the area where many evacuees from eastern Aleppo were transported for testing, receiving assistance, medical care, and other humanitarian assistance.

The United Nations' conclusion, therefore, was that more than 100 victims of such executions could have been identified. How many people died this way during this period, or how many are still waiting for the same fate? Risk of execution or arrest is a danger facing many others in the besieged areas of Syria, and the fate of others may be similar at each agreement on a local truce between the opposition and the government, upon returning areas to government control.[125]

This explains why the United Nations has publicly[126] refused to participate in the "evacuation" operations in Aleppo, as was done previously in Homs. Such "evacuation" operations are just forcible displacement, which is a crime against humanity per international law.

The Independent International Commission of Inquiry established by Human Rights Council concludes in its report on displacement

> that fierce battles in Aleppo, northern Homs, Damascus, Rif Dimashq and the governorates of Daraa and Idlib have led to massive displacement of more than 1 million Syrian men, women, and children within six months. In the majority of cases documented by the Commission, displacement was directly caused by the wrongful conduct of the warring parties. This behavior included, on the one hand, unlawful attacks that forced civilians to flee their homes in a state of fear and despair. And, on the other hand, clandestine displacements pursuant to "evacuation agreements" negotiated between the warring parties and reached as part of local truces. While continuing to document aerial and ground attacks that kill and maim scores of civilians throughout the country, the Commission notes that, after seven years of war, more than five and a half million refugees have fled the country and more than six and a half million civilians are living as displaced persons within Syrian Arab Republic.[127]

The fear of returning to an area where unlawful behavior of the belligerents caused the flight of people from their homes, will also have a devastating impact on the future demography of Syrian society, a society that is now dangerously torn. In its report, the Committee in many cases adds accounts from individuals who fear to return to areas that have recently been recaptured by government forces, including in Eastern Ghouta (Rif Dimashq), the northern Rif Homs, and the Yarmouk Camp (Damascus). Large-scale looting of civilian homes has taken place, and looters didn't leave much for civilians who fled to avoid clashes. In other cases, internally displaced persons have found that their homes have been occupied by combatants and their families and have been used for military purposes.[128]

In 2016, The term "useful Syria" became popular in the press, after Russian President Putin used it many times.[129] It refers to the governorates of Damascus, Rif Dimashq, Homs, Hama, Tartous, and Lattakia.[130] This area is of strategic importance to the Syrian regime as it includes most of the rich governorates in Syria as well as the capital, Damascus. These are provinces inhabited by a majority of the pro-regime Alawite minority, and provide access to the Mediterranean Sea. This reveals the great influence of the regime in these governorates and guarantees their permanent loyalty and rule out any demonstrations or protests aimed at radical political reforms or aimed at altering the structure of the political system that has been in place since 1970.

The "Useful Syria" holds a strategic significance to key regime allies in Russia, Iran, and Hezbollah, as it is a crucial link in the geographic chain between Tehran and Iraq, andHezbollah in eastern and southern Lebanon, the area Jordanian King Abdullah described as the Shiite crescent. They greatly support the significant regional impact of what they call the "axis of resistance," facilitate the exchange of goods and weapons, and ensure long-range regional influence.

There is increased anecdotal public reporting that there will be re-engineering of the demographics of Syria after the war on sectarian grounds. There are reports that the Shia from Lebanon, Iran, and Iraq, as well as Alawites and Shiites from other regions of Syria, have been granted Syrian nationality.[131] They also will be transferred to refill areas that were targets of strategic displacements. This began early in 2013 when Hezbollah expelled residents from al-Qusayr near the border with Lebanon and its environs after a two-week siege and repopulated the area with Shiite Lebanese and Syrian families.[132]

There were talks about establishing new regulatory bodies to supervise Shia religious festivals and to carry out Shia rituals.[133] The targeted areas also saw the construction of several new Shiite shrines after the fall of Homs, which was reported to have overseen the rebuilding of the originally Sunni "Abu Jaafar al-Tayyar" mosque, which was reconstituted in the traditional Shiite architectural style.[134]

Many writers go on to focus on what they call "demographic shift" based on "sectarian foundations," especially in the Rif Dimashq and Homs governorates, where one writer states that "the Sunni population has decreased by 49 percent in Rif Dimashq, while the number of Shiites has increased 13 times. In Homs Governorate, more than 80 percent of the Sunni population has been displaced or expelled, while the number of Shiites has increased seven times, and the number of Alawites has increased by slightly less than 50 percent compared to 2011 estimates."[135] Of course, it is impossible to confirm these numbers and there is no scientific way to make sure that this is true because there are no statistics on the sectarian level in Syria and therefore these figures appear to be random. This is despite our recognition of cases that have been confirmed concerning the granting of Syrian nationality or the Syrian national ID to fighters of Iraqi, Afghani, and Pakistani Shiite militias who fought with the Assad regime. The regime relied on them due to lack of human resources, with significant defections within the governmental army, but it is difficult to prove this large number.

In my opinion, it seems clear that the Syrian regime has sought to reformulate the demographics of certain areas of Syria (and continues to do so) and this is likely to mean that a large number of refugees and internally displaced populations (IDPs) will most likely not be able to return to their homes. This is not based on sectarian grounds, but on the basis of politics and political loyalty to the regime. The seizure of housing, land, and property may have made the return of refugees difficult in practical and economic terms. In addition, the demographic engineering that is taking place is likely to make it almost impossible for many Syrians, who fled or were expelled from the country, to return, especially those who fled the areas that were formerly controlled by the opposition and those from the affected provinces.

Moreover, it is estimated that 1.5 million Syrians are wanted by the Syrian intelligence services,[136] many of them adult men who are perceived as traitors because they have escaped forced recruitment. There have been reports of many returning refugees, who face arrest, torture, and even execution because they are suspected of belonging to opposition groups or because they have escaped forced recruitment.[137]

It can therefore be said that Assad's strategy of forced displacement is based on political rather than sectarian lines and will ultimately lead to a demographic shift that everyone seems convinced is becoming a reality representing Syria, which is today controlled by Aasad.

FIFTH: DENIAL OF RETURN FOR ASYLUM SEEKERS THROUGH THE DESTRUCTION OF PRIVATE PROPERTY

Not all wars are associated with asylum as we have always known it, but inevitably there is an exodus within the country. If these IDPs cross into the borders of another country, the displaced people become refugees. The Syrian war was characterized as the fuel for millions of refugees to flee not only to the neighboring countries of Lebanon, Jordan, Iraq, and Turkey, but also to different countries of Europe and East Asia. While the refugee crisis in Europe escalated in 2015, refugee quotas were distributed to different European countries, so Syrian families arrived in Iceland, for example, although most Syrians had not heard of this country or thought about going there.

After examining factors that drove refugees to flee their homeland and leave their houses and take refuge, we had talked about these factors combined in detail such as indiscriminate shelling, intensive use of barrel bombs, use of chemical weapons, blockade, etc. Here we will talk about the factors that are transforming Syrian refugees into permanent residents in host countries. The refugee loses the right to return to his country because of a number or arsenal of security laws and procedures and the destruction of property that makes such return to his homeland impossible.

Displacement of populations from targeted areas are often followed by the seizure of displaced persons' lands, dwellings, and properties by regime forces. Issuing of forged documents is a widespread tactic of transferring legal ownership of property and land from their rightful owners to loyalists of the regime. There have also been reports of the deliberate destruction of civil registries in Homs, [138] and formerly opposition-held areas in Rif Dimashq, Homs, and Aleppo, as well as confiscation of documents at checkpoints. [139]

LAWS RESTRICTING THE RETURN OF DISPLACED PERSONS

Theft, Looting, and Destruction of Private Property

The internet is filled with astonishingly clear video clips depicting the act of theft and looting of the property of others [140] in the name of the National Defence Militia and other pro-regime militias or members of the regime's Syrian army. The regime also openly destroyed buildings and large tracts of land under the pretext of land zoning. Human Rights Watch documented that

> as of July 2012, Syrian authorities deliberately demolished thousands of residential buildings and, in some cases, entire neighborhoods, using explosives and bulldozers, in Damascus and Hama, which are two of the largest cities in Syria. Government officials and pro-government media outlets claimed that the demolitions had taken place as part of urban planning efforts to remove illegal buildings. However, the demolitions were carried out under the supervision of military forces and were often carried out following fighting between government forces and the opposition in those areas. These circumstances, in addition to witness statements and more honest statements by government officials reported by the media, point to the attachment of demolitions to armed conflict, in contravention of international humanitarian law or the laws of war. [141]

Human Rights Watch concluded that seven of the large-scale demolitions documented in its report contravene the laws of war, because they did not serve any necessary military purpose, it seemed that were intended to punish the civilian population, or because they caused disproportionate damage to civilians. The first large-scale demolition cases documented by Human Rights Watch occurred in July 2012. Satellite photos analyzed by the organization show that the Syrian authorities have since demolished a total of 140 hectares or the equivalent of 200 football pitches, mostly from residential buildings, in seven neighborhoods in Hama and Damascus. Many of the buildings were houses that were built up for several floors, some of which were eight floors. Thousands of families have lost their homes as a result of these demolitions. [142]

Government authorities also demolished residential buildings in the areas of Al-Tadamon and al-Qaboun immediately after government forces responded to a military attack by the opposition in the capital in mid-July 2012. Opposition fighters were also alleged to have used two residential neighborhoods in Hama, which were destroyed by government forces in September and October 2012, and April and May 2013, to enter and exit the city. Some demolitions were carried out within the scope of government military or strategic targets that were attacked by opposition forces, such as Mazzeh Military Airport, Damascus International Airport, and theTishreen military hospital in the Barzeh neighborhood. Although the actions taken by the authorities to protect these military or strategic objectives may have been justified, the destruction of hundreds of residential buildings, in some cases within kilometers of those targets, appears to have been disproportionate and contrary to international law. [143]

Some government and military officials openly demonstrated the true cause of the demolitions. The governor of Rif Dimashq, Hussein Makhlouf, openly declared in a media interview in October 2012 that demolitions were necessary to expel opposition fighters. After the demolition of Wadi al-Joz in Hama in May 2013, the army warned residents in other neighborhoods that their homes would also be demolished if opposition fighters attacked government forces from those neighborhoods, according to a witness from a nearby neighborhood. [144]

Of course, the Assad regime continued with complete demolitions of entire neighborhoods for purely political reasons based on support for the Syrian revolution, as was done in Homs, Darayya, and other areas.

The regime has also carried out a complete and extensive survey and falsification of property records throughout the country in order to prevent the population from returning and claiming any rights. On July 1, 2013, for example, regime forces bombed the land registry of the central city of Homs, resulting in a massive fire that destroyed many property records in the city, prompting city residents to believe that it was intentional "because it was the only structure that burned in the safest part of the city." [145] Instances of burning of land registries in both Zabadani, Darayya, Daraa, and Al-Quseir have also been recorded. The burning of records not only prevents original landlords from recovering their property but also allows for the transfer of ownership to pro-regime individuals and groups.

In some cases, the destroyed records also included electricity and water bills that could be used to prove ownership, and there were many accounts of falsification of records, including the use of forged documents to carry out the sale and transfer of ownership to new owners.[146]

These procedures, coupled with the promulgation of laws and decrees, may be seen as "attempts" to reform real estate laws and accelerate reconstruction under the war, but do not take into account the situation of displaced or missing persons. Some people consider these actions deliberate as they were designed to target them and prevent them from returning through confiscating their property and denying them the right to own property.

Decree No. 66 of 2012

The regime has also used more "institutional" tactics, such as the promulgation of Decree No. 66 of 2012, which allowed the government to initiate legal land grabbing in several areas adjacent to Damascus.[147] Worse still, Presidential Decree 19/2012 on combating terrorism allows the state to confiscate the property of persons convicted of a wide range of crimes.[148] Legislative Decree No. 63 of 2012 allows the Syrian minister of finance to nationalize the assets and property of anyone subject to the Anti-Terrorism Act of 2012, which has a very broad definition of what constitutes terrorism.

Decree No. 12 of 2016

The regime has used legal tools to legitimize these transfers of property and make them permanent. Decree No. 12 of 2016 calls for the digitization of land registration throughout Syria, which has the apparent objective of erasing past ownership and formalizing the illegal transfers mentioned above.[149] Because of the large-scale destruction and falsification of property registers, the new digital property registry will permanently erase all records of the past, formalizing the seizure of property in such a way as to make it difficult, if not impossible,[150] to undo it in the future. There are also reports that the streets in the targeted areas are given new names, in order to further confuse anyone claiming any property that has been illegally transferred.[151]

Law 33 of 2017

Act No. 33 of 2017 allows any claimant to claim ownership of any uninhabited property. The claimant only needs proofing witnesses as evidence and approval by the relevant administrative body, to make the ownership legally binding.[152]

Law No. 10 of 2018

Although Law No. 10 of 2018 has received unprecedented international attention, it is only a continuation of this strategy. Regardless of the previous model in which local councils have greater authority over the areas they represent, the new law gives the regime the power to establish "regulatory zones" to oversee and manage reconstruction processes.[153] Law No. 10 of 2018 is a slightly modified version of Legislative Decree No. 66 of 2012. This act states that any subject in the Syrian constitution may be regulated by law—after it is submitted to the People's Assembly or by a legislative decree issued under article 113 of the 2012 constitution, or even by a regulatory decree from the executive branch.

Law No. 10 can be read and interpreted only with consideration of legislation (laws and legislative and regulatory decrees) that have been issued in Syria for half a century on expropriation and urban planning, which in turn do not include minimum standards for the protection of owner's rights. In this law there is sufficient reference to successive expropriation laws, as well as the famous Law No. 60 of 1979, in addition to the bureaucratic regulatory and administrative context entrusted with enforcing such legislation. In some of its provisions, Act No. 10 referred to some of this legislation for enforcement.[154]

Law No. 10 grants to Syrians only 30 days to register their ownership of any property located within one of these newly established areas, after which any unclaimed property will be nationalized. In the event that the owners show proof of ownership of the property in the regulatory area, they will get shares in the area.[155] As is clear, Law No. 10 will be used to take advantage of large-scale absences and the displaced populations' inability to resort to court.[156]

Although Law No. 10 allows registration of ownership by a legal representative or relative, it is probable that many persons will not be able to provide sufficient evidence of ownership due to destruction and confiscation of the above-mentioned registries. Also, other measures are taken to prevent any specific reasons that are used by individuals who may be forced to submit ownership claims.[157]

Human Rights Watch notes that IDPs, especially those fleeing from areas deemed anti-government, are more likely to have their property confiscated under Law No. 10. According to the United Nations refugee agency, more than 11 million Syrians have been displaced or have taken refuge in host countries since the beginning of the Syrian conflict. Many displaced Syrians will not be able to return to their properties to file the claim themselves. At the same time, the 30-day limit for a relative or legal agent to submit a claim on his behalf will be a short period for many.[158] Seventy percent of refugees also lack basic identification documents, according to the Norwegian Refugee Council.[159] These documents are necessary for filing a request for proof of ownership and for the appointment of a legally recognized agent.

By July 2017, one-third of the houses in Syria had been destroyed. The law does not provide for compensation or any other measure for those whose property has been destroyed. It would be impossible for the thousands who had been forcibly disappeared during the conflict to claim the missing person's property. These persons were unable to submit their own applications for proof of ownership or to appoint a legally recognized agent. In many cases, their relatives would not be able to show why the owners could not make the request themselves. In addition, relatives of persons in detention may not have the necessary documentation to prove the missing person's death, and since the property is still owned by the missing person, they will not be able to apply for proof of ownership.[160]

The requirement for security clearance of a local agent for the property owner who is traveling or whose whereabouts are unknown will constitute a barrier. Residents of areas controlled by anti-government groups are unlikely to apply for or be able to obtain a security clearance.[161]

Moreover, many of those who have been displaced from areas that were held by the opposition are likely to be afraid even of trying to claim ownership of their property—personally or through an agent—because of the fact that they are likely to be seen as affiliated with opposition groups. This is particularly true for those formerly in opposition-controlled areas who have been subjected to forced displacement or displacement campaigns.

After Law No. 10 received many criticisms from the international community,[162] the Syrian regime announced that it was in the process of amending the law and extending the deadline for property claims from 30 days to one year.[163] While this amendment may relieve pressure on some owners, it is unlikely to change anything for those who are subject to the regime's strategy of expropriation and displacement, and if the owners still have documents proving their ownership, they are unlikely to be ready to apply or to claim their property for fear of persecution.

The seizure of large amounts of property serves several purposes of the regime. First, it gives it the ability to fund and strengthen Assad's governmental army and begin the reconstruction process. Secondly, it allows Bashar al-Assad to reward military leaders, businessmen, and politicians who have supported his regime throughout the war, either financially, or with property or contracts for reconstruction and development. The acquisition of property is likely to enrich the capitalists aligned with the regime. It will also stimulate foreign investment, which will be vital if reconstruction costs are to be met.[164]

Thirdly, large-scale displacements and seizure of property also give the regime means to control who returns and where they should be located (e.g.,

Assad and his allies are able to engineer the demographics of postwar Syria as they see fit).

NOTES

1. Syrian Central Bureau of Statistics. "المكتــب المركــزي للإحصـــاء," Cbssyr.Sy, 2019, cbssyr.sy/index-EN.htm.

2. "Worldometers," Worldometers.Info, 2019, www.worldometers.info/faq/. As per CBS, the population of Syria back in 2018 increased to reach 25,000,000, but this is an inaccurate number. However, CBS indicates that this number includes Syrians in general, not only those located in Syrian lands.

3. United Nations, "Syria Emergency," UNHCR, Apr. 19, 2018, www.unhcr.org/syria-emergency.html . The UNHCR states the registered Syrians do not constitute the whole number of Syrian refugees. Despite the fact that registration protects the refugees against forced relocation and forced detention and grants them the chance to reach services and receive aid as well as facilitating their independent movement, not all neighboring countries have allowed the registration of refugees. The registration of the refugees includes the details of the grounds on which they sought refuge, which is an essential requirement to draw a line between refugees, emigrants, and those seeking relocation instead of being sent back to their countries. We may argue that the number of Syrian refugees has exceeded five million; which we shall tackle later on.

4. Caroline A. Hartzell, *Mixed Motives? Explaining the Decision to Integrate Militaries at Civil War's End*, in Roy Lickleder (ed.), *New Armies from Old: Merging Competing Military Forces After Civil Wars* (Washington, DC: Georgetown University Press, 2014), 13–27.

5. Mark Gersovitz and Norma Kriger, "What Is a Civil War? A Critical Review of Its Definition and (Econometric) Consequences," *The World Bank Research Observer*, May 2013, 159–190. Mark Gersovitz and Norma Kriger argue that the civil wars are considered "civil" in respect to the factors and the regional impacts that get involved in the course of such wars and affect their outcomes.

6. According to the assessments of the Human Rights Data Analysis Group (HRDAG), the number of those killed due to the Syrian dispute till April 2014 has reached 191,369. This report is based on the data provided by seven Syrian human rights organizations as well as the data issued by the Syrian regime. HRDAG released its third report commissioned by the UN OHCHR on the reported killings in the Syrian conflict. HRDAG identified 191,369 deaths from the start of the conflict in March 2011 to April 2014. See: Updated Statistical Analysis of Documentation of Killings in the Syrian Arab Republic, August 2014; see the link at https://hrdag.org/wp-content/uploads/2014/08/HRDAG-SY-UpdatedReportAug2014.pdf. Later, the UN OHCHR didn't assign anyone to prepare any reports on surveying the number of dead. Hence, all data provided are approximate data of the Syrian organizations as well as the documentation center www.dchrs.org and the Syrian Network for Human Rights (http://sn4hr.org) operating in the field of documentation, and the Damascus Center for Human Rights Studies. Check violations at http://vdc-sy.net/en/.

7. Also, check the site documenting violations in Cambodia: http://www.d.dccam.org. Bruce Sharp, "Counting Hell," see the link at: http://www.mekong.net/cambodia/deaths.htm. Refer to the report issued by the CIA, titled "Cambodia: A demographic catastrophe," released back in 1980, tackling the perilous demographic shifts created by the Khmer Rouge regime due to displacement operations, killings, and tortures. This information can be compared to the Syrian case. See CIA, "Kampuchea: A Demographic Catastrophe." Research for this report was completed on the 17th of January 1980. See the link at http://www.mekong.net/cambodia/demcat.htm . Also see: "The Number—Quanitifying Crimes Against Humanity in Cambodia," Documentation Center of Cambodia, Phnom Penh, Cambodia, 1999. See the link at http://www.mekong.net/cambodia/toll.htm.

8. Marijke Verpoorten, "The Death Toll of the Rwandan Genocide: A Detailed Analysis for Gikongoro Province," *Population*, 2005/4 (Vol. 60), 331–367. Also see the report "Rwanda: Death, Despair and Defiance," August, 1995.

9. Damien McElroy, "Syrian Regime Deploys Deadly New Weapons on Rebels," *The Telegraph*, August 31, 2012; see the link at https://www.telegraph.co.uk/news/worldnews/middleeast/syria/9512719/Syrian-regime-deploys-deadly-new-weapons-on-rebels.html.

See the first video showing barrel bombs: "Syrian Regime Forces Filmed Dropping 'Barrel Bomb' on Homs," *Telegraph*, September 1, 2012, https://www.telegraph.co.uk/news/world-news/middleeast/syria/9514698/Syrian-regime-forces-filmed-dropping-barrel-bomb-on-Homs.html.

In his book *Syria: A Way of Suffering to Freedom*, Dr. Azmi Besharah recalls that there were three milestones that led the Syrian regime to employ air force weapons in July 2012: the assassination of the officers of the Syrian Crisis Management Cell in the National Security building, the armed opposition entrance into Aleppo, and the third Veto used by Russia and China in the Security Council against a Western proposal calling on placing Anan's plan under the UN seventh chapter. All these factors combined and made the Syrian regime seek the air force to bombard rebellions in various Syrian areas, where it employed military helicopters in battles in Damascus and Aleppo back in July 2012. Later, it employed such weapons constantly. See Azmi Besharah, *Syria: A Way of Suffering to Freedom* (Doha: Arabic Center for Research and Political Studies, 2013), 260–261

10. Major Keith J. Stalder, "The Air War in Afghanistan," Global Security, January 25, 1985; see the link at https://www.globalsecurity.org/military/library/report/1985/SKJ.htm; also, see Alan Taylor, "The Soviet War in Afghanistan, 1979–1989," the *Atlantic*, August 4, 2014; see the link at https://www.theatlantic.com/photo/2014/08/the-soviet-war-in-afghanistan-1979–1989/100786/.

11. Gideon S. Hall, Major, "Warlords of the Somali Civil War (1988–1995)," Air Command and Staff College Air University, A Research Report, Maxwell Air Force Base, Alabama, April 2015.

Follow the testimony of one of the officers, who refused to bombard civilians.

Former Somali Air Force Pilot, who refused to bomb civilians, "Somaliland," see the link at http://www.somalilandsun.com/somaliland-former-somali-air-force-pilot-who-refused-to-bomb-civilians-in-hargiesa/. The last visit to the site was on June 17, 2019.

12. Human Rights Watch, War Crimes in Chechnya and the Response of the West, Testimony before the Senate Committee on Foreign Relations, February 29, 2000; see the link at https://www.hrw.org/news/2000/02/29/war-crimes-chechnya-and-response-west.

During his testimony before the American Senate, Peter Pokharit from HRW recalls that air raids have turned most of Chechnya into a desert. Most war reporters mentioned that they have never witnessed such destruction as what they witnessed in Grozny. The Russian army used fuel-operated bombs and highly destructive explosives that had the ability to destroy the ground fortifications civilians sought to escape the war. This has led to civil causalities as the fuel bombs left a smoke cloud creating a fatal shock wave. Explosions managed to kill people hiding in trenches, buildings, caves, or shelters.

Robyn Dixon, "Russia Strikes Chechnya with Fuel-Air Bombs," *Los Angeles Times*, December 28, 1999 see the link at http://articles.latimes.com/1999/dec/28/news/mn-48358.

It's worth mentioning that the Russian air force has used the same bombs later against civilians in Aleppo in 2016. See the HRW report. Human Rights Watch, Russia/Syria: War Crimes in Month of Bombing Aleppo, December 1, 2016, see the link at https://www.hrw.org/news/2016/12/01/russia-syria-war-crimes-month-bombing-aleppo.

13. Human Rights Watch, "Death from the Skies: Deliberate and Indiscriminate Air Strikes on Civilians," April 10, 2013; see the link at https://www.hrw.org/report/2013/04/10/death-skies/deliberate-and-indiscriminate-air-strikes-civilians.

The organization kept documenting the periodical employment of the barrel bombs in various reports, as they were used by the Syrian regime back in 2015 as a means of collective punishment against the civilians without having any military targets to hit/achieve. As the human factor kept waning within the lines of the Syrian governmental army due to divisions and refusal of many youth to recruit, the Syrian regime's ability to regain the areas falling out of its control has become impossible. As compensation, the barrel bombs were excessively used as a means of collective punishment for all the areas falling under the control of the opposition.

14. Human Rights Watch, "Syria: Unlawful Air Attacks Terrorize Aleppo: New Evidence of Government Barrel Bombs Despite UN Resolution," March 24, 2014; see the link at https://www.hrw.org/news/2014/03/24/syria-unlawful-air-attacks-terrorize-aleppo; see also: Human Rights Watch, "Syria: New Barrel Bombs Hit Aleppo: Attacks Defy UN, Hit Medical Facilities," April 28, 2014, https://www.hrw.org/news/2014/04/28/syria-new-barrel-bombs-hit-aleppo.

Weapons Law Encyclopedia, Barrel Bombs, see the link at http://www.weaponslaw.org/glossary/barrel-bomb. Last visit to site August 5, 2018. The encyclopedia adds that: some barrel bombs may include what can be classified as prohibited weapons as per international laws. In addition, such barrel bombs that are used as a weapon of war, especially within civilians gathering spots or near such spots, do violate IHL regarding accuracy and discrimination as well as discriminating between civilians and fighters.

15. Human Rights Watch, "Syria: Barrage of Barrel Bombs, Attacks on Civilians Defy UN Resolution," July 30, 2014, https://www.hrw.org/news/2014/07/30/syria-barrage-barrel-bombs, Also see: Human Rights Watch, "Syria: New Spate of Barrel Bomb Attacks: Government Defying UN Resolution," February 24, 2015, https://www.hrw.org/news/2015/02/24/syria-new-spate-barrel-bomb-attacks.

16. Amnesty International, "Syria: 'Death Everywhere'—War Crimes and Human Rights Abuses in Aleppo, Syria," MDE 24/1370/2015, May 5, 2015, https://www.amnesty.org/en/documents/mde24/1370/2015/en/.

17. Debarati Guha-Sapir, Benjamin Schlüter, Jose Manuel Rodriguez-Llanes, Louis Lillywhite and Madelyn Hsiao-Rei Hicks, "Patterns of Civilian and Child Deaths Due to War-Related Violence in Syria: A Comparative Analysis from the Violation Documentation Center Dataset, 2011–16," *The Lancet*, Volume 6, PE103–E110, January 1, 2018.

18. Debarati Guha-Sapir, Benjamin Schlüter, Jose Manuel Rodriguez-Llanes, Louis Lillywhite, and Madelyn Hsiao-Rei Hicks, "Patterns of Civilian and Child Deaths," January 1, 2018.

19. Debarati Guha-Sapir, Benjamin Schlüter, Jose Manuel Rodriguez-Llanes, Louis Lillywhite, and Madelyn Hsiao-Rei Hicks, "Patterns of Civilian and Child Deaths," January 1, 2018. The report stated that the VDC recorded 143,630 conflict-related violent deaths with complete information between March 18, 2011, and December 31, 2016. Syrian civilians constituted 101,453 (70.6 percent) of the deaths compared with 42,177 (29.4 percent) opposition combatants. Direct deaths were caused by wide-area weapons of shelling and air bombardments in 58,099 (57.3 percent) civilians, including 8,285 (74.6 percent) civilian women and 13,810 (79.4 percent) civilian children, and in 4,058 (9.6 percent) opposition combatants. Proportions of children among civilian deaths increased from 8.9 percent (388 of 4,254 civilian deaths) in 2011 to 19 percent (4,927 of 25,972) in 2013, and to 23.3 percent (2,662 of 11,444) in 2016. Of 7,566 deaths from barrel bombs, 7,351 (97.2 percent) were civilians, of whom 2,007 (27.3 percent) were children. Of 20,281 deaths by execution, 18,747 (92.4 percent) were civilians and 1,534 (7.6 percent) were opposition combatants. Compared with opposition child soldiers who were male (n=333), deaths of civilian male children (n=11,730) were caused more often by air bombardments (39.2 percent vs 5.4 percent, p<0.0001) and shelling (37.3 percent vs 13.2 percent, p<0.0001) and less often by shooting (12.5 percent vs 76.0 percent, p<0.0001).

20. Jeremy Bowen, "Assad Is Firm in Defending His Actions in BBC Interview," B.B.C., February 10, 2015. See the link at https://www.bbc.co.uk/news/world-middle-east-31311896, and for the full interview see the link at https://www.bbc.com/news/av/world-middle-east-31327153/syria-conflict-bbc-exclusive-interview-with-president-bashar-al-assad.

The BBC-renowned journalist, who interviewed Assad, stated that this reply is "rude" and mentioned that the barrel bombs "are the most commonly used weapons in the Regime's arsenal."

21. Philippe Bolopion, "Barrel Bombs Are No Laughing Matter, President Assad," Human Rights Watch, February 10, 2015, https://www.hrw.org/news/2015/02/10/dispatches-barrel-bombs-are-no-laughing-matter-president-assad.

22. "Security Council Unanimously Adopts Resolution 2139 (2014) to Ease Aid Delivery to Syrians, Provide Relief from 'Chilling Darkness'," Security Council, SC/11292, February 22, 2014, https://www.un.org/press/en/2014/sc11292.doc.htm.

23. See the full text of resolution 2139 (2014) at https://www.un.org/press/en/2014/sc11292.doc.htm.

24. Human Rights Watch, "Syria: New Spate of Barrel Bomb Attacks: Government Defying UN Resolution," February 24, 2015, https://www.hrw.org/news/2015/02/24/syria-new-spate-barrel-bomb-attacks.

25. Amnesty International, "Syria: Terrifying Eyewitness Video of Life Under Siege and Barrel Bombs Must Spur Humanitarian Lifeline," April 19, 2016, https://www.amnesty.org/en/press-releases/2016/04/syria-terrifying-eyewitness-video-of-life-under-siege-and-barrel-bombs/, and Lucy Westcott, "Barrel Bombs Rain Down on Syria's Besieged Daraya," *Newsweek*, April 18, 2016, https://www.newsweek.com/daraya-syria-barrel-boms-amnesty-international-449160.

You can watch the method of dropping these barrel bombs over Darayya that led to the wide-ranging displacement of its residents via HQ authenticated videos via the following links:

https://www.youtube.com/watch?v=6UUFecNzLV4
https://www.youtube.com/watch?v=xv5FR9na9EU
https://www.youtube.com/watch?v=XxfbvhMAT_k

26. Under-Secretary-General for Humanitarian Affairs and Emergency Relief Coordinator, Stephen O'Brien: Statement to the Security Council on Syria, New York, June 23, 2016, UN Office for the Coordination of Humanitarian Affairs, June 23, 2016, https://reliefweb.int/report/syrian-arab-republic/under-secretary-general-humanitarian-affairs-and-emergency-relief-42.

27. Kenneth Roth, "To Stem the Flow of Syrian Refugees, Stop the Barrel Bombs," Human Rights Watch, September 23, 2015 https://www.hrw.org/news/2015/09/23/stem-flow-syrian-refugees-stop-barrel-bombs.

28. Independent International Comission of Iquiry on the Syrian Arab Republic, "Sieges as a Weapon of War: Encircle, Starve, Surrender," May 29, 2008, https://www.ohchr.org/Documents/HRBodies/HRCouncil/CoISyria/PolicyPaperSieges_29May2018.pdf.

29. Independent International Commission of Inquiry on the Syrian Arab Republic, 10th Report of Commission of Inquiry on Syria (A/HRC/30/48), August 13, 2015 (published on September 3, 2015), https://www.ohchr.org/en/hrbodies/hrc/iicisyria/pages/documentation.aspx.

30. Independent International Comission of Inquiry on the Syrian Arab Republic, "Sieges as a Weapon of War: Encircle, Starve, Surrender," May 29, 2008, 3.

31. Muhammad Jamal Parout, *The Last Decade of the History of Syria* (Doha: Arabic Center for Research and Political Studies, 1st Ed., 2012), page 253.

32. Anthony Shadid, "Syria Escalates Crackdown as Tanks Go to Restive City," *New York Times* (April 25, 2011), https://www.nytimes.com/2011/04/26/world/middleeast/26syria.html.

33. "Syria Protests: Rights Group Warns of 'Deraa Massacre,'" B.B.C News, May 5, 2011, https://www.bbc.co.uk/news/world-middle-east-13299793, and Damascus Center for Human Rights Studies (DCHRS), Daraa: Ten Days of Massacres, Washington D.C, May 2011, see the link at https://www.fidh.org/IMG/article_PDF/article_a9590.pdf.

34. Physicians for Human Rights, Access Denied: UN Aid Deliveries to Syria's Besieged and Hard-to-Reach Areas, New York: Physicians for Human Rights, March 2017.

35. Syrian American Medical Society (SAMS), Slow Death: Life and Death in Syrian Communities under Siege, March 2015, https://www.sams-usa.net/wp-content/uploads/2016/09/Slow-Death_Syria-Under-Siege.pdf.

36. First Quarterly Report on Besieged Areas in Syria, PAX, The Syria Institute, February 2016, https://siegewatch.org/wp-content/uploads/2015/10/PAX-RAPPORT-SIEGE-WATCH-FINAL-SINGLE-PAGES-DEF.pdf.

37. Syrian American Medical Society (SAMS), March 2015.

38. Security Council Endorses Syria Cessation of Hostilities Accord, Unanimously Adopting Resolution 2268 (2016), SC/12261, February 26, 2016, https://www.un.org/press/en/2014/sc11292.doc.htm .

39. First Quarterly Report on Besieged Areas in Syria, PAX, The Syria Institute, February 2016.

40. The AFP reported on the devastating conditions that Darayya's children have been going through for four consecutive years under siege and isolated from the outer world. Amna (38 years) mother of Yazzan, who was born during the siege, after four hours of arriving at a temporary accommodation center in the village of Hargalah, says: "My son Yazzan doesn't know what biscuits or ice-cream is! Every time he sees them he gets thrilled," she adds while wearing a black coat in the heat. "He picked up the piece of bread and kissed it. He was thrilled with the ice cream and asked me if such is some kind of sweets." Shyly, she says "When he saw the biscuits, he went out of his mind; how couldn't he!"

Yazzan is one of Darayya's children, who were born after the Syrian regime siege back in 2012 of the city located in Damascus's Western Ghouta. These children were raised in devastating conditions as they faced a shortage of food supplies and bread for four years, as reported by the AFP. It adds: "While Amna was talking to the AFP reporter, Yazzan came in holding a bag of grind prepared hummus and asked her about it. She replied to Yazzan and told him that it was 'msabbaha.' He asked if it was edible, and when she confirmed that it was, he held the bag close to his heart and kissed it. "We used to eat a single meal of soup at sunset and we had to wait for the following sunset to receive our next meal." Amna clarified that they had no power or gas. "My heart was torn to watch my kid hungry and I cried because I had nothing to feed him. He used to cry and seek neighbours for food." As a result of the excessive bombardment the city has witnessed, Amna's family had to remain in the shelter for long periods. Amna also told us that she couldn't send her kids to school like other mothers did as she feared for them. The AFP has reported another story similar to Yazzan's, as Huda's (30 years) children saw fruits for the first time in the years since the siege. Huda said, "My two boys (3 and 5 years) were surprised to see tomatoes for the first time. They were even shocked to see bread." The AFP concludes its report stating that despite the devastating conditions, Huda didn't wish to leave her city as she couldn't rent a house; however, she said "Now, we have no choice; we either leave the place or live under bombardment." She also stated that she brought some stones from Darayya as "a souvenir" in hopes that one day they may return." See "Children of the Siege in Darayya Discover Biscuits and Ice Cream," Al-Quds Al-Arabi Newspaper, London: August 27, 2016, http://www.alquds.co.uk/?p=588404.

41. First Quarterly Report on Besieged Areas in Syria, PAX, The Syria Institute, February 2016.

42. Security Council Demands 30–Day Cessation of Hostilities in Syria to Enable Humanitarian Aid Delivery, Unanimously Adopting Resolution 2401 (2018), SC/13221, February 24, 2018, https://www.un.org/press/en/2018/sc13221.doc.htm .

A few days following the negotiations held at the Security Council, Russia managed to delay the issuance of the resolution and edited its formula to prevent the condemnation of Assad's regime. Instead of the formula submitted by Sweden and Kuwait, Russia rejected the inclusion of any phrases that may condemn Assad's regime and hold it liable for the killing of the civilians in Ghouta. However, even with a less strongly worded resolution, the Syrian regime did not implement the articles of the resolution as it did with previous ones. The Syrian regime went on with its military campaign against Ghouta and it was supported by the Russian forces. The campaign against Ghouta ended up with the evacuation of the all militants and most civilians. Although Nikki Haley—the United States Ambassador to the United Nations—used harsh language threatening to seek procedures outside of the Security Council, if the latter failed to guarantee the implementation of the 2401/2018 resolution demanding all parties to cease warlike acts immediately and for a period of 30 consecutive days, in order to allow aid and humanitarian assistance to be delivered and to allow unhindered and constant medical evacuation in the light of international law, such resolution remained ineffective and meaningless in Ghouta, where bombs and shells were still used and lands were open for the expansion of Assad's militias to control the remaining parts of Ghouta.

43. Syrian American Medical Society (SAMS), Thirteen Targeted Attacks on Hospitals in East Ghouta in 48 Hours. Medics Describe the Situation as "Catastrophic," February 20, 2018, https://www.sams-usa.net/press_release/thirteen-targeted-attacks-hospitals-east-ghouta-48–hours-medics-describe-situation-catastrophic/

?utm_source=All+Subscribersandutm_campaign=136a3c7e45–EMAIL_CAMPAIGN_2018_0 2_01andutm_medium=emailandutm_term=0_ed72e8fdb0–136a3c7e45–81768241.

44. The Assad regime managed to control Eastern Ghouta fully after dividing it into three parts: Arbin, Haresta, and Douma. While holding an agreement to evacuate the fighters in Arbin and Haresta to Idlib, Douma kept resisting for a couple of days.

45. Amnesty International, 'Left To Die Under Siege' War Crimes and Human Rights Abuses in Eastern Ghouta, Syria (London: Amnesty International, 2015).

46. Amnesty International, 'Left To Die Under Siege,' (London: Amnesty International, 2015).

47. Amnesty International, 'Left To Die Under Siege,' (London: Amnesty International, 2015).

48. Syrian American Medical Society (SAMS), Slow Death, March 2015.

49. The Syrian regime forces disapproved the full deliverance of humanitarian aid as it only allowed a few vehicles into the besieged areas in order to manipulate international resolutions and stated that the Syrian regime did not allow the UN human relief convoys to enter, although the regime was aware of the fact that such vehicles would not be adequate to help more than 400,000 civilians, who were still living in Eastern Ghouta. The residents of the area realized that they would not be allowed to live there anymore, even if they had lived under siege for the last five years. Now, they had to go with the last option of all: either displacement or death.

50. Will Todman, Sieges in Syria: Profiteering from Misery, MEI Policy Focus 2016–14, Washington, D.C.: Middle East Institute, June 2016.

51. Following three years of forcing the city residents to leave their houses and villages unwillingly, the Syrian regime couldn't allocate more than 2 million dollars to remove the wrecks and ruins produced by its own bombardments. This amount was allocated during the meeting of the Syrian cabinet on . . . where the cabinet approved the amount of one billion Syrian pounds (equal to approximately 2 million dollars) in order to remove the wrecks and ruins produced by the four-year constant bombardment of the city. The amounts paid to destroy the city are way more than that; the city was hit by almost 40,000 barrel bombs as per the data issued by the UN! The regime had also promised the return of 300,000 of the city's residents to secure the basic services for the city including water, power, etc.

52. Syria Humanitarian Assistance Response Plan, January 1–June 30, 2013, UN Office for the Coordination of Humanitarian Affairs, December 19, 2012, https://reliefweb.int/report/ syrian-arab-republic/fact-sheet-syria-humanitarian-assistance-response-plan-1–january- 30–june.

53. Waleed Alfares, Homs: Documentation of 700 Days of Siege (Doha: Arabic Center for Research and Political Studies, 2015), pages 62–63.

54. Waleed Alfares, Homs: The Big Siege: Documentation of 700 Days of Siege, page 63.

55. Security Council Unanimously Adopts Resolution 2139 (2014) to Ease Aid Delivery to Syrians, Provide Relief from 'Chilling Darkness,' SC/11292, February 22, 2014, https://www. un.org/press/en/2014/sc11292.doc.htm .

56. "Hard to reach areas," the phrase preferred by the Syrian regime, has been constantly used in the UN data instead of "under siege" because the latter is disapproved by the Syrian regime, even as the UN holds the regime constantly liable.

57. Security Council Unanimously Adopts Resolution 2139 (2014) to Ease Aid Delivery to Syrians, Provide Relief from 'Chilling Darkness,' SC/11292, February 22, 2014.

58. Independent International Commission of Inquiry on the Syrian Arab Republic, "Sieges as a Weapon of War: Encircle, Starve, Surrender," May 29, 2008, 3–4.

59. Todd A. Salzman, Rape Camps as a Means of Ethnic Cleansing: Religious, Cultural, and Ethical Responses to Rape Victims in the Former Yugoslavia, *Human Rights Quarterly*, Vol. 20, No. 2 (May 1998), 348–378.

60. Todd A. Salzman, Rape Camps as a Means of Ethnic Cleansing, *Human Rights Quarterly*, Vol. 20, No. 2 (May 1998), 348–349.

61. Human Rights Watch, Kosovo: Rape as a Weapon of "Ethnic Cleansing," Human Rights Watch report, March 1, 2000; see the report at https://www.hrw.org/report/2000/03/01/kosovo- rape-weapon-ethnic-cleansing.

62. Meredeth Turshen, "The Political Economy of Rape: An Analysis of Systematic Rape and Sexual Abuse of Women During Armed Conflict in Africa," in *Victors, Perpetrators or Actors: Gender, Armed Conflict and Political Violence*, edited by C. Moser and F. Clarke, 55–68, London: Zed Books, 2001.

63. Meredeth Turshen, The Political Economy of Rape, 56.

64. Sonja C. Grover, *Child Soldier Victims of Genocidal Forcible Transfer: Exonerating Child Soldiers Charged With Grave Conflict-Related International Crimes*, Springer Science and Business Media, 2012.

65. Jameel Alhassan, Elimination shall be the fate of those, who spoke, participated and kept silent . . . Syrian Reporter website, check the following link: https://syrian-reporter.net/ %D8%AE%D8%A7%D8%B5–%D8%AC%D9%85%D9%8A%D9%84–%D8%A7%D9%84 %D8%AD%D8%B3%D9%86–%D8%A7%D9%84%D8%AA%D8%B5%D9%81%D9%8A% D8%A9–%D9%85%D8%B5%D9%8A%D8%B1–%D9%83%D9%84–%D9%85%D9%86–% D9%82%D8%A7%D9%84–%D9%88/.

Regardless of the validity or invalidity of such a statement, live interviews with Jameel Alassan indicated his use of those same terms and adoption of the same dogma. Check Alhassan's interviews with Robert Fisk, the British journalist, in which the former stated that the implementation of more violent measures from the very beginning could have saved Syria long years of war: Robert Fisk, Tougher Tactics Would Have Ended Syrian War, Claims the Country's Top Intelligence General, *The Independent*, November 27, 2016, see the link at https://www.independent.co.uk/news/world/middle-east/syria-war-aleppo-exclusive-top-syrian-general-robert-fisk-tougher-tacts-a7442161.html.

66. Ahmed Rahal, the head of the civil registry in Syria, declared that 100,000 deaths were recorded from the early days of 2017 to August 2018. He indicated that such records didn't include the cause of death as such were approved official death certificates sent by the regime to the civil registry departments regarding detainees who died from torture inside prisons without indicating the cause of death. Rahal also told "Alwattan" Newspaper—the pro-Assad newspaper owned by Rami Makhlouf—that on Thursday, September 8, 2018, the civil registry recorded the deaths of 32,000 people during 2018, in addition to 68,000 during 2017, without indicating the causes of death. He added that the civil registry records the deaths under any document issued by the regime-affiliated departments. He stated that on recording such cases, no mention was made if the deceased was missing or killed by torture. In a rare confession of the elimination of 100,000 political detainees under torture. See the transcript of the interview in "Alwattan" Newspaper using the following link: http://alwatan.sy/archives/162101.

67. Kheder Khaddour, The Alawite Dilemma (Homs 2012), published in *Playing the Sectarian Card Identities and Affiliations of Local Communities in Syria*, edited by Friederike Stolleis, Beirut: Friedrich-Ebert-Stiftung, 2015, 12.

68. No Return to Homs: A Case Study on Demographic Engineering in Syria, PAX, The Syria Institute, February 2017, 16; see the link at http://syriainstitute.org/2017/02/21/no-return-to-homs-a-case-study-on-demographic-engineering-in-syria/.

69. Government Paramilitary Forces, Paramilitary Forces of Bangladesh, Paramilitary Forces of India, Paramilitary Forces of Iraq, General Books, 2011.

70. The Syrian Network for Human Rights defines the sectarian massacres as "massacres of a unique pattern that can be revealed in the killings committed; as the attacking contradictory forces don't only shoot their victim to death; however, they tend to carry out other practices and behaviours such as slaughtering whole families including women, men and children, burning and mutilating bodies, rapes and sexual assaults, and looting and house burning. These are crimes that have a sectarian or an ethnic background." The Syrian Network for Human Rights: Holocaust Community: The most hideous massacres that hold sectarian or ethnic patterns in Syria, June 2015; see the full report via: http://sn4hr.org/public_html/wp-content/pdf/arabic/ Holocaust_community.pdf. I think that this definition focuses on the "hideousness" of the act more than the identity of the doer and his motives.

71. The Syrian Network for Human Rights: Holocaust Community: The most hideous massacres that hold sectarian or ethnic patterns in Syria, June 2015.

72. Azmi Besharah, *Syria: A Way of Suffering to Freedom: A Current Attempt* (Doha: Arabic Center for Research and Political Studies, 2013), 108–118; Waleed Alfares, *Homs: The Big Siege, Documentation of 700 Days of Siege*, 25.

73. No Return to Homs: A Case Study on Demographic Engineering in Syria, PAX, The Syria Institute, February 2017, 16.

74. Azmi Besharah, *Syria: A Way of Suffering to Freedom*, 119–122; Waleed Alfares, *Homs: The Big Siege*, 27.

75. Waleed Alfares, *Homs: The Big Siege*, 42.

76. Waleed Alfares, *Homs: The Big Siege*, 43.

77. The analysis of Human Rights Watch described the severe attacks that targeted the residential areas in Baba Amr as well as the government's refusal to grant civilians safe exit from the area as most of the suburb buildings were turned into ruins by March 2012. Later, sieging, targeting civilians, and destroying infrastructure had become the three main mechanisms applied by the government to force civilians to exit Homs and the remaining areas falling under the control of the rebellions during the siege and the destruction of Baba Amr, thus displacing approximately 50,000–60,000 of its residents. See Human Rights Watch, "Razed to the Ground: Syria's Unlawful Neighborhood Demolitions in 2012–2013," New York, January 30, 2014. Reports state that the number of victims has reached more than 200m who were killed due to the employment of shells targeting the area. See Matthew Weaver, "Battle for Baba Amr—Timeline: Key Dates in the Fight between the Syrian Regime and Rebel Forces for the Baba Amr District of Homs," The Guardian, March 1, 2012, https://www.theguardian.com/world/2012/mar/01/battle-baba-amr-timeline-syria.

78. Azmi Besharah, *Syria: A Way of Suffering to Freedom*, 335.

79. Azmi Besharah, *Syria: A Way of Suffering to Freedom*, 335.

80. Azmi Besharah, *Syria: A Way of Suffering to Freedom*, 336; Waleed Alfares, *Homs: The Big Siege*, 37; The Syrian Network for Human Rights: Holocaust Community: The most hideous massacres that hold sectarian or ethnic patterns in Syria, June 2015, 6.

81. Human Rights Watch, "In Cold Blood: Summary Executions by Syrian Security Forces and Pro-Government Militias," New York: Human Rights Watch, April 9, 2012. See the link at https://www.hrw.org/report/2012/04/09/cold-blood/summary-executions-syrian-security-forces-and-pro-government-militias.

82. Azmi Besharah, *Syria: A Way of Suffering to Freedom*, 336; Waleed Alfares, *Homs: The Big Siege*, 38; The Syrian Network for Human Rights, Holocaust Community: The most hideous massacres that hold sectarian or ethnic patterns in Syria, June 2015, 6.

83. Human Rights Watch, "In Cold Blood," April 9, 2012.

84. Martin Chulov and Mona Mahmood, The Houla massacre: Reconstructing the Events of May 25, Interviews with Survivors Reveal the Full Story of the Bloody Horror that Left More Than 100 Syrians Dead, The Guardian, June 1, 2012, https://www.theguardian.com/world/2012/jun/01/houla-massacre-reconstructing-25–may.

85. Report of the Independent International Commission of Inquiry on the Syrian Arab Republic, Human Rights Council, Twenty-Fifth Session, Oral Update of the Commission of Inquiry on the Syrian Arab Republic (Al-Houlah report), June 26, 2012; see the link at https://www.ohchr.org/Documents/HRBodies/HRCouncil/RegularSession/Session20/COI_OralUpdate_A.HRC.20.CRP.1.pdf.

86. Report of the Independent International Commission of Inquiry on the Syrian Arab Republic, 10.

87. The Syrian Network for Human Rights, Holocaust Community: The Most Hideous Massacres that Hold Sectarian or Ethnic Patterns in Syria, June 2015, 6–9. See the full report here: http://sn4hr.org/public_html/wp-content/pdf/arabic/Holocaust_community.pdf.

88. Marie Forestier, "You Want Freedom? This Is Your Freedom": Rape as a Tactic of the Assad Regime, Center of Women, Peace and Security, March 2017, http://eprints.lse.ac.uk/69475/1/Forestier_You_want_freedom_this_is_your_freedom_WP3_2017.pdf.

89. Marie Forestier, "You Want Freedom? This Is Your Freedom," Center of Women, Peace and Security, March 2017, 11.

90. Rob Grace, With Internal Displacement on the Rise, International Law Leaves Protection Gap, Harvard Humanitarian Initiative, May 14, 2015, http://atha.se/blog/internal-displacement-rise-international-law-leaves-protection-gap.

91. The Pinheiro Principles: United Nations Principles on Housing and Property Restitution for Refugees and Displaced Persons, Geneva: Center on Housing Rights and Evictions, 2009. Also, see: Handbook on Housing and Property Restitution for Refugees and Displaced Persons: Implementing the "Pinheiro Principles", OCHA, March 2007. See the report at this link: https://www.ohchr.org/Documents/Publications/pinheiro_principles.pdf.

92. Economic, Social And Cultural Rights, Housing and Property Restitution in the Context of the Return of Refugees and Internally Displaced People, Final Report of the Special Rapporteur, Paulo Sérgio Pinheiro. Commission on Human Rights, Sub-Commission on the Promotion and Protection of Human Rights, Fifty-sixth session, E/CN.4/Sub.2/2005/17, June 28, 2005. See the link at http://www.unhcr.org/protection/idps/50f94d849/principles-housing-property-restitution-refugees-displaced-persons-pinheiro.html.

93. The Pinheiro Principles, Geneva: Center on Housing Rights and Evictions, 2009. See the link at https://2001–2009.state.gov/documents/organization/99774.pdf.

94. Assad Regime Confiscating Homes of Millions of Syrian Refugees Abroad, Informed Comments, April 28, 2018, https://www.juancole.com/2018/04/confiscating-millions-refugees.html.

95. Urban Research Center, IMAR: Reconstruction report, http://urc-sy.com/en/wp-content/uploads/2017/01/170120–IMAR-En-No3–Rev07.pdf. Of course, there are thousands of videos documenting the so-called "Ta'feesh" operations all over the Syrian cities that were controlled by the regime. For instance, see the following link on YouTube: https://www.youtube.com/watch?v=9xn5jhMrIBk.

The following report documents the Ta'feesh operations in Haresta and Eastern Ghouta following the Syrian regime taking control over such areas in May 2018, https://www.youtube.com/watch?v=p3uHJjKEINs.

96. For more information about the pro-government militant groups, Shabiha in particular, see the chapter written by Reynolds in the following book: *The Alawis of Syria: War, Faith and Politics in the Levant* (Urban Conflicts, Divided Societies), edited by Michael Kerr and Craig Larkin, Oxford University Press (first edition), 2015.

97. The residents of Darayya were granted conditional return (after obtaining the approval of the security authorities) in August 2018 (i.e., three years after the Syrian regime lost control over the city). The city was entered by 1,000 out of 300,000 (city residents before 2011). The residents exchanged horrifying videos of the looting and burning of houses which made the return decision an impossible one, especially in the light of an official disclaimer of liability and compensation. See the issue of the "Enab Baladi" newspaper issued in Darayya by activists, who documented all the phases of displacement as well the return of the city residents, via the following link: https://www.enabbaladi.net/archives/250875.

98. Homs Agreement mediated by the UN, February 7, 2014. The full transcript of the Agreement at the researcher's.

99. UN Habitat Syria, Neighborhood Profile: Old City of Homs, June 2014, https://unhabitat.org/neighbourhood-profile-old-city-of-homs/.

100. No Return to Homs: A Case Study on Demographic Engineering in Syria, PAX, The Syria Institute, February 2017, 24.

101. Amnesty International, We Leave or We Die: Forced Displacement Under Syria's "Reconciliation" Agreements, Index: MDE 24/7309/2017, December 2017, 48–59, https://www.amnesty.org/download/Documents/MDE2473092017ENGLISH.pdf.

102. Amnesty International, We Leave or We Die, December 2017, 54–55.

103. Amnesty International, We Leave or We Die, December 2017, 56.

104. Amnesty International, We Leave or We Die, December 2017, 56–57.

105. No Return to Homs, PAX, The Syria Institute, February 2017, 24.

106. UNHCR, Minimum Standards for Participation in Humanitarian Inter-Agency Evacuations Informed by International Humanitarian and International Human Rights Law, February 13, 2014; see the link at http://www.refworld.org/docid/57a97e0b4.html.

107. No Return to Homs, PAX, The Syria Institute, February 2017, 24.

108. Amnesty International, We Leave or We Die, December 2017, 34–47.

109. Amnesty International, We Leave or We Die, December 2017, 45–47.

110. Security Council Resolution 2328 adopted by the Security Council at its 7841st meeting, on December 19, 2016, http://www.un.org/en/ga/search/view_doc.asp?symbol=S/RES/2328(2016).

111. Ben Taub, Aleppo's "Evacuation" Is a Crime Against Humanity, *New Yorker*, December 22, 2016, https://www.newyorker.com/news/daily-comment/aleppos-evacuation-is-a-crime-against-humanity.

112. Rome Statute of the International Criminal Court, Text of the Rome Statute circulated as document A/CONF.183/9 of July 17, 1998, and corrected by process-verbaux of November 10, 1998, July 12, 1999, November 30, 1999, May 8, 2000, January 17, 2001, and January 16, 2002. The Statute entered into force on July 1, 2002. See the full text at https://www.icc-cpi.int/nr/rdonlyres/ea9aeff7–5752–4f84–be94–0a655eb30e16/0/rome_statute_english.pdf.

113. Ben Taub, Aleppo's "Evacuation" Is a Crime Against Humanity, The New Yorker, December 22, 2016.

114. Patrick Wintour, UN to Ask Syria to Approve Airdrops of Humanitarian Aid, The Guardian, June 3, 2016, https://www.theguardian.com/world/2016/jun/03/un-to-ask-syria-ap-prove-airdrops-humanitarian-aid.

115. Kheder Khaddour, Consumed by War: The End of Aleppo and Northern Syria's Political Order, October 2017. See the report at this link: http://library.fes.de/pdf-files/iez/13783.pdf.

116. Atlantic Council, Breaking Aleppo, Washington, D.C.: Atlantic Council, 2017; see the link at http://www.publications.atlanticcouncil.org/breakingaleppo/.

117. Azmi Bishara, Russian Intervention in Syria: Geostrategy Is Paramount, Doha: Arab Center for Research and Policy Studies, November 2015; see the link at https://www.dohainstitute.org/en/lists/ACRPS-PDFDocumentLibrary/Rus-sian_Intervention_in_Syria_Geostrategy_is_Paramount.pdf; Endre Szénási, Russian Military Intervention in Syria: The Rebirth of Russian Military Might, Hungarian Ministry of Defense: Defense Policy Department, 2015; S. R. Covington, The Meaning of Russia's Campaign in Syria, Harvard Kennedy School: Belfer Center for Science and International Affairs, December 2015; Markus Kaim and Oliver Tamminga, Russia's Military Intervention in Syria Its Operation Plan, Objectives, and Consequences for the West's Policies, Berlin: German Institute for International and Security Affairs, November 2015; Thomas Pierret, Syria in the Aftermath of the Russian Intervention: The Paradoxes of De-Confliction, Dossier: Geopolitical Turmoil and Its Effects in the Mediterranean Region, Mediterranean Yearbook 2017, 122–126; Salam Al-saadi, Russia's Military Involvement in Syria: An Integrated Realist and Constructivist Approach, *International Journal of Law, Humanities and Social Science*, Volume 1, Issue 5 (September 2017), 87–93; Woodrow Wilson School of Public and International Affairs, Policy Workshop Final Report, Princeton University, January 2018.

118. Atlantic Council, Breaking Aleppo: Evacuation, Washington D.C.: Atlantic Council, 2017, http://www.publications.atlanticcouncil.org/breakingaleppo/evacuation/.

119. Siege Watch Fifth Quarterly Report on Besieged Areas in Syria, November 2016–January 2017, PAX, The Syria Institute, May 2017, https://siegewatch.org/wp-content/uploads/2015/10/pax-tsi-siege-watch-5–final-r.pdf.

120. Atlantic Council, Breaking Aleppo: Evacuation, Washington D.C.: Atlantic Council, 2017, http://www.publications.atlanticcouncil.org/breakingaleppo/evacuation/.

121. Atlantic Council, Breaking Aleppo: Evacuation, Washington D.C.: Atlantic Council, 2017, http://www.publications.atlanticcouncil.org/breakingaleppo/evacuation/.

122. Atlantic Council, Breaking Aleppo: Evacuation, Washington D.C.: Atlantic Council, 2017, http://www.publications.atlanticcouncil.org/breakingaleppo/evacuation/.

123. Atlantic Council, Breaking Aleppo: Evacuation, Washington D.C.: Atlantic Council, 2017, http://www.publications.atlanticcouncil.org/breakingaleppo/evacuation/.

124. U.S Government: State Department, Human Rights Report, 2017, see the link at https://www.state.gov/reports/2017–country-reports-on-human-rights-practices/ .

125. Atlantic Council, Breaking Aleppo: Evacuation, Washington D.C.: Atlantic Council, 2017, http://www.publications.atlanticcouncil.org/breakingaleppo/evacuation/.

126. UN Human Rights Chief "Appalled" by Faltering Aleppo Evacuation Deal, Voice of America (VOA) News, December 14th, 2016; see the link at https://www.voanews.com/a/aleppo-evacuation-civilians-rebels/3635600.html; also, see: U.N. Calls for Aleppo Evacuation Plan; Politician Warns of Extermination, Reuters, December 8, 2016, https://www.reuters.com/article/us-mideast-crisis-syria-aleppo-un-idUSKBN13X1DM.

127. UN Commission of Inquiry on Syria: Unparalleled Numbers of Syrians Displaced in under Six Months, Report of the Independent International Commission of Inquiry on the Syrian Arab Republic, Human Rights Council, Thirty-ninth session, September 10–28, 2018. See the report at this link: https://www.ohchr.org/EN/HRBodies/HRC/Pages/NewsDetail.aspx?NewsID=23541&LangID=E.

128. UN Commission of Inquiry on Syria: Unparalleled Numbers of Syrians Displaced in under Six Months, Report of the Independent International Commission of Inquiry on the Syrian Arab Republic, Human Rights Council, Thirty-ninth session, September 10–28, 2018. See the report at this link: https://www.ohchr.org/EN/HRBodies/HRC/Pages/NewsDetail.aspx?NewsID=23541&LangID=E.

129. Samuel Charap and Jeffrey Martini, Trump Should Strike a Deal with Putin on Syria, *Foreign Policy*, July 10, 2018, see the link at https://foreignpolicy.com/2018/07/10/trump-should-strike-a-deal-with-putin-on-syria/.

130. Hussain Ibrahim Qutrib, "Useful Syria" and Demographic Changes in Syria, King Faisal Center for Research and Islamic Studies.

131. In his article posted in "Alnahar" Newspaper, the writer, Ahmed Ayyash, mentioned that according to diplomatic figures "Bashar al-Assad has granted around two million National ID Cards to Iranians as well as to members of Quds Force—affiliated to Iran's Revolutionary Guard including Hezbollah and their families. He added that "they were not only given such cards; they were also allowed to dwell in the areas that were emptied after the displacement of their residents in Ghouta and its Rif, Homs, Hama and Aleppo."

See: Assad Rewards Hezbollah and Iran's Revolutionary Guard by Granting Syrian Nationality to Two Million Shiites, Alwattan Newspaper, June 2018. The news was widely spread without any proof to establish such massive number. It seems that this number was fueled by sectarian intentions.

132. Hezbollah Shows Off Its Capacities and "Control" over AlQuseir—Syria , Alsharq Alawsat Newspaper, Novermber 15, 2016, https://aawsat.com/home/article/784711/%C2%AB%D8%AD%D8%B2%D8%A8-%D8%A7%D9%84%D9%84%D9%87%C2%BB-%D9%8A%D8%B3%D8%AA%D8%B9%D8%B1%D8%B6-%D9%82%D9%88%D8%AA%D9%87-%D9%88%C2%AB%D8%B3%D9%8A%D8%B7%D8%B1%D8%AA%D9%87%C2%BB-%D9%81%D9%8A-%D8%A7%D9%84%D9%82%D8%B5%D9%8A%D8%B1-%D8%A7%D9%84%D8%B3%D9%88%D8%B1%D9%8A%D8%A9-%D9%88%D8%B3%D8%B7-%D8%B5%D9%85%D8%AA-%D9%84%D8%A8%D9%86%D8%A7%D9%86%D9%8A.

133. The Shiite Presence in Damascus and Attempts to Change Its Demography, Orient News, July 20, https://orient-news.net/ar/news_show/89121/0/.

134. Iranian Visit to Place the Cornerstone Turning Abu Jaafar al-Tayyar Mosque into a Shiite Shrine, Zaman Alwasl, June 11, 2015, https://www.zamanalwsl.net/news/article/50686.

135. Jesse Thompson, Syria's Shifting Sands: Demographic Engineering and Refugee Return, Middle East Institute for Research and Strategic Studies, June 6, 2016, http://meirss.org/1262-2/; and see: Sinan Hatahet and Ayman Aldassouky, Forced Demographic Changes in Syria, Al-Sharq Forum paper series, Alsharq Forum, September 2017.

136. A million and a half are wanted by the Assad regime. Zaman Alwasl, https://leaks.zamanalwsl.net/1.5m.php.

137. More than half a million are wanted by the Syrian regime to join the Army, Zaman Alwasl, https://leaks.zamanalwsl.net/matlobeen.php.

138. No Return to Homs, PAX, The Syria Institute, February 2017, 24.

139. Jihad Yazigi, Destruct to Reconstruct: How the Syrian Regime Capitalizes on Property Destruction and Land Legislation, Friedrich Ebert Stiftung, July 2017. See the full report at http://library.fes.de/pdf-files/iez/13562.pdf.

140. Videos can be reviewed on the Syrian Archive website, a database for the violations as documented in motion. The website has managed to collect more than 1,520,763 videos, 4,442 of which were investigated. All investigated videos include a full documentation. See: https://syrianarchive.org/en.

141. Human Rights Watch, Razed to the Ground: Syria's Unlawful Neighborhood Demolitions in 2012–2013, January 30, 2014; see the full report at https://www.hrw.org/report/2014/01/30/razed-ground/syrias-unlawful-neighborhood-demolitions-2012-2013.

142. Human Rights Watch, Razed to the Ground, January 30, 2014, 3–4.

143. Human Rights Watch, Razed to the Ground, January 30, 2014, 15–26.

144. Human Rights Watch, Razed to the Ground, January 30, 2014, 29.

145. Jihad Yazigi, Destruct to Reconstruct, Friedrich Ebert Stiftung, July 2017, 6.

146. No Return to Homs, PAX, The Syria Institute, February 2017, 24.

147. Human Rights Watch, Razed to the Ground, January 30, 2014, 5–12.

148. UN Commission of Inquiry on Syria: Unparalleled Numbers of Syrians Displaced in under Six Months, Report of the Independent International Commission of Inquiry on the Syrian Arab Republic, Human Rights Council, Thirty-ninth session, September 10–28, 2018, 22.

149. Jesse Thompson, Syria's Shifting Sands: Demographic Engineering and Refugee Return, Middle East Institute for Research and Strategic Studies, June 6, 2016; see the link at https://www.meirss.org/syrias-shifting-sands-demographic-engineering-and-refugee-return/.

150. No Return to Homs, PAX, The Syria Institute, February 2017, 32.

151. Jesse Thompson, Syria's Shifting Sands, Middle East Institute for Research and Strategic Studies, June 6, 2016.

152. Jesse Thompson, Syria's Shifting Sands, Middle East Institute for Research and Strategic Studies, June 6, 2016.

153. Arab Reform Initiative, Law No. 10 on Reconstruction: A Legal Reading of Organized Mass Expropriation in Syria, Policy Paper, June 2018. See the full report at https://www.arabreform.net/en/node/1312.

154. Arab Reform Initiative, Law No. 10 on Reconstruction, Policy Paper, June 2018.

155. Human Rights Watch, Syria's New Property Law, May 29, 2018; see the link at https://www.hrw.org/news/2018/05/29/qa-syrias-new-property-law.

156. Human Rights Watch, Syria's New Property Law, May 29, 2018; see the link at https://www.hrw.org/news/2018/05/29/qa-syrias-new-property-law.

157. Arab Reform Initiative, Law No. 10 on Reconstruction, Policy Paper, June 2018.

158. Human Rights Watch, Syria's New Property Law, May 29, 2018; see the link at https://www.hrw.org/news/2018/05/29/qa-syrias-new-property-law.

159. Samer Aburass, Syrian Refugees' Documentation Crisis, Norwegian Refugee Council, January 2017, https://www.nrc.no/news/2017/january/syrian-refugees-documentation-crisis/.

160. Human Rights Watch, Syria's New Property Law, May 29, 2018; see the link at https://www.hrw.org/news/2018/05/29/qa-syrias-new-property-law.

161. Human Rights Watch, Syria's New Property Law, May 29, 2018; see the link at https://www.hrw.org/news/2018/05/29/qa-syrias-new-property-law.

162. Germany submitted a bill to the General Assembly of the United Nations to decline this law.
        Germany Urges UN to Block Recently Introduced Law No. 10, April 28, 2018, http://en.etilaf.org/all-news/political-news/germany-urges-un-to-block-recently-introduced-law-no-10.html.

163. The Syrian Foreign Minister, Walid Muallem, announced an amendment to a controversial urban planning law in Syria that would extend the month-long deadline for citizens to prove their ownership under the threat of confiscation. See: Muallem Comments on Law No.10 that Was Internationally Criticized, RT, June 2, 2018. See https://arabic.rt.com/middle_east/947944-%D8%A7%D9%84%D9%85%D8%B9%D9%84%D9%85-%D8%A7%D9%84%D9%82%D8%A7%D9%86%D9%88%D9%86-%D8%B1%D9%82%D9%85-10-%D9%83%D8%A7%D9%86-%D8%B6%D8%B1%D9%88%D8%B1%D8%A9-%D8%A3%D8%B9%D8%A8%D8%A8%D8%AA-%D8%A7%D8%B3%D8%AA%D8%B9%D8%A7%D8%AF%D8%A9-%D8%A7%D9%84

%D8%BA%D9%88%D8%B7%D8%A9–%D9%84%D8%A5%D8%B9%D8%A7%D8%AF%
D8%A9–%D8%A7%D9%84%D9%85%D9%85%D8%AA%D9%84%D9%83%D8%A7%D8
%AA-%D9%84%D8%A3%D8%B5%D8%AD%D8%A7%D8%A8%D9%87%D8%A7/.

164. Jesse Thompson, Syria's Shifting Sands, Middle East Institute for Research and Strategic Studies, June 6, 2016.

Naame Shaam Report: Silent Sectarian Cleansing: The Iranian Role in Mass Demolitions
and Population Transfers in Syria, May 2015, http://www.naameshaam.org/report-silent-sectar-
ian-cleansing/index.html.

Chapter Three

Forced Evacuations

In the Syrian Context

David M. Crane

The purpose of this chapter is to illustrate the boundaries of forced evacuations in the context of a non-international armed conflict. Specifically, in the case of the Syrian civil war we will examine what international humanitarian laws apply and what conclusions can be drawn regarding the instances of evacuations in the city of Aleppo and the Damascus suburb of Darayya.

OVERVIEW

The Syrian civil war originated with peaceful protests in March 2011 after 15 boys were detained and tortured for graffiti supporting the rash of protests across the Middle East known as the Arab Spring. The Syrian government responded to protests violently, which only prompted more protesting. As tensions and violence escalated, members of the Syrian military began to defect and formed the Free Syrian Army with the goal of overthrowing the Assad Regime.[1]

Foreign nations, various terrorist organizations, and rebel groups have been involved since the beginning of the conflict. The conflict has become a complex scenario for international actors as well as for Syrian nationals. It is kaleidoscopic in scope. Where one thing changes everything changes. There are at least nine major factions of armed groups fighting in Syria. Fighting generally on the side of the Syrian Regime are: Syrian Armed Forces, Al-Quds Force and Basji Militia, National defense forces and allied paramilitary groups, and Hezbollah. These groups fighting with the Syrian regime are also supported by Russia and Iran. Major factions of the rebel forces include: the

Islamic Front, Jabhat Al-Nusra, the so-called Islamic State, and the Free Syrian Army. The United States has been involved with supporting the Free Syrian Army, and other moderate rebel groups. However, the U.S. has also been fighting the so-called Islamic State in Iraq and northern Syria with the cooperation and support of other nations. Moreover, the United States and other nations have been attempting to degrade and destroy Al-Qaeda and its' affiliates. Jabhat Al-Nusra has been historically linked with Al-Qaeda, and therefore been targeted by the United States and others. Finally, the YPG, or the Popular Protection Units, has been seen as independent and fighting against factions on either side.[2]

NON-INTERNATIONAL ARMED CONFLICT

Under the laws of armed conflict, or international humanitarian law, a threshold distinction must be made between two types of conflict. The conflict must either fall within the category of international armed conflict or non-international armed conflict.

International armed conflict is defined by the Geneva Conventions of 1949 Common Article 2 as "declared war or of any other armed conflict which may arise between two or more of the High Contracting Parties, even if the state of war is not recognized by one of them. The Convention shall also apply to all cases of partial or total occupation of the territory of a High Contracting Party, even if the said occupation meets with no armed resistance."[3] In the case of the Syrian conflict there are indeed several contracting parties or nations participating. However, there has been very careful attention paid to not engage one another. Russian and Iranian forces are working with Syrian regime forces. The United States has not quarreled with any of these forces preventing the conflict from becoming an international armed conflict. Therefore, the Syrian conflict does not fit within this definition.

Non-International Armed Conflicts are defined in Common Article 3 of the 1949 Geneva Conventions as well as Article 1 of Additional Protocol II (AP II). The two sources define non-international armed conflict differently and apply differing rules to each definition.

Common Article 3 states non-international armed conflict is "armed conflicts not of an international character occurring in the territory of one of the High Contracting Parties." This definition seems to capture most forms of hostilities and violence. Moreover, it is worth noting that since the universal ratification of the Geneva Conventions the territorial requirement has lost significance. It is virtually impossible for any armed conflict between a government and a non-governmental armed group to take place outside of a contracting party's territory.

To narrow the focus of common Article 3 and exclude less serious forms of violence it has been generally accepted that the lower standard of Article 1 of AP II should be applied. This lower standard is usually considered in two parts. First, "the hostilities must reach a minimum level of intensity. This may be the case, for example, when the hostilities are of a collective character or when the government is obliged to use military force against the insurgents, instead of mere police forces."[4] Second, "non-governmental groups involved in the conflict must be considered as 'parties to the conflict', meaning that they possess organized armed forces. This means for example that these forces have to be under a certain command structure and have the capacity to sustain military operations."[5] In the Syrian case, the protracted conflict between government and rebel groups with bitter and extremely violent battles over cities and territories illustrates that the conflict has surpassed the Common Article 3 standard.

Article 1 of AP II itself applies a stricter standard for when conflicts rise to meet the classification of non-international armed conflict. Article 1 states that the instrument will apply to conflicts that "take place in the territory of a High Contracting Party between its armed forces and dissident armed forces or other organized armed groups which, under responsible command, exercise such control over a part of its territory as to enable them to carry out sustained and concerted military operations and to implement this Protocol."[6] This first requires territorial control of the parties. Next, it demands the conflict be between rebel groups and government forces. This definition excludes application to conflicts between warring rebel groups. In the case of Syria, the conflict has risen to the Article 1 standard. The battles between Syrian regime forces and rebel groups for cities like Aleppo, and neighborhoods like Darayya outside of Damascus, evidence that the armed groups fighting the government forces have exercised requisite control over territory to carry out sustained and concerted military operations.

Forced Evacuations of Aleppo and Darayya

Aleppo, at one time the economic hub and most populated city in Syria,[7] split in two when rebel armed groups—having overrun Government forces—captured its' eastern half in 2012.[8] Syrian Government forces, unable to dislodge the rebel groups alone,[9] worked in conjunction with the Russian Federation to cut supply lines,[10] encircle eastern Aleppo,[11] and enlist national militias.[12] Thus began the siege of eastern Aleppo. Following the cutting off of Castello Road from eastern Aleppo by Government forces, Russia declared a "humanitarian operation" which it claimed opened three safe routes to allow the voluntary evacuation of civilians.[13] The Victims Documentation Center explains that "witness accounts documented by local activists confirmed targeting civilians who tried to evacuate by snipers and forbidding them crossing to the Government-controlled areas."[14] Since the siege's start, the VDC claims to have documented 3,497 civilian deaths.[15]

Evacuations began on December 15, 2016.[16] The Red Crescent and Red Cross observed the execution of negotiated terms of the evacuation process, detailing that for each bus leaving eastern Aleppo, a bus would leave Kafrayya and Foa'a.[17] This agreement was renegotiated and executed again on the 19th of December; this new agreement detailed "(1) Phase one: to evacuate 1,250 people from Kefria and Foa'a and half the people in eastern Aleppo. (2) Phase two: to evacuate another 1,250 and finalize eastern Aleppo's evacuation. (3) Phase three: Evacuate the remaining 1,500 people in Kefria and Foa'a and 1,500 from Madaya and Zabadani."[18]

As the United Nations has noted:

> After the Government reached an evacuation agreement with armed groups in mid-December, residents of eastern Aleppo were transported from the city in government buses and private vehicles to Idlib, while others fled to western Aleppo. None has the option to remain in their home. As part of the agreement, more than 1,000 people were evacuated from Foah and Kafraya and went to Aleppo, Tartous, Homs and Latakia governorates.

It is because the belligerents have evacuated eastern Aleppo for strategic reasons, and not for any imperative military necessity or for the security of civilians, that this evacuation amounts to the war crime of forced displacement.

Darayya would be considered a suburb of the Syrian capital city of Damascus. Darayya was at one time a city with around 200,000 inhabitants.[19] The city had held out against the regime's medieval siege warfare tactics for four years.[20] Darayya is emblematic of the Syrian civil war in that it was one of the initial places of protest during the Arab Spring.[21] It was here that rebel forces popped up and expelled regime forces only miles away from the Presidential Palace.[22] It also became a messy conflict area. Rebel forces more than likely shelled civilians living in Damascus.[23] For four years the rebels held out in the city of Darayya.[24] For most of that time, rebels were utilizing smuggling routes and tunnels to supply fighters as well as civilians living in the city.[25] However, the regime closed off the routes being used, stopped the flow of supplies to the city, and began a siege campaign.[26] As the fighters as well as civilians began to starve, the regime continued to bombard the city, destroying field hospitals and other necessities.[27] In May 2016 the UN sent a fact finding mission to Darayya. Officials were followed around by hundreds of malnourished women and children.[28] The Government had repeatedly denied access to aid organizations and convoys.[29] When given permission, aid convoys are turned around due to bombardment and shelling.[30] In August 2016, Rebel and Government forces pieced together a deal. Rebels agreed to hand over control of Darayya and the regime would allow safe passage out of the surrounded city.[31] Some civilians have fled with rebels to northern parts of the country, while others moved to an area closer to Damascus where they are being sheltered and screened by the regime.[32] The civilians who have fled with the rebels have said they have done so out of fear of the regime.[33] Reports state that around 700 fighters were evacuated from Darayya with the approximately 4,000 remaining civilians.[34]

PRINCIPLES OF THE LAWS OF ARMED CONFLICT

International Humanitarian Law describes the *jus in bello*, laws concerning the conduct of warfare.[35] This body of law aims "to protect persons who are not or are no longer taking part in hostilities, the sick and wounded, prisoners and civilians, and to define the rights and obligations of the parties to a conflict in the conduct of hostilities."[36]

This body of law is typically broken down into four principles.[37] First among these is that of military necessity.[38] The Hague Convention preamble states "military necessity has been taken into account in framing the regulations, and has not been left outside to control and limit their application."[39] Oppenheim explains the second principle as that of humanity[40], which is sometimes explained as the avoidance of unnecessary suffering or that violence that is not essential for the defeat of a belligerent is not permitted.[41] A third principle of discrimination ensures the respect for and protection of the civilian population and civilian objects.[42] Schindler and Toman explain that Article 48 directs parties to the conflict to, at all times, ensure discrimination between "the civilian population and combatants and between civilian objects and military objectives and accordingly shall direct their operations only against military objects."[43] A civilian is "any person who does not belong to one of the categories of persons referred to in Article 4 . . . of the Third Convention [GPW] and in article 43 of this Protocol."[44] Additional Protocol I, Art. 51(b) spells out the final principle. Proportionality, is defined in the Protocol as "an attack which may be expected to cause incidental loss of civilian life, injury to civilians, damage to civilian objects, or a combination thereof, which would be excessive in relation to the concrete and direct military advantage anticipated."[45]

The 1987 commentary on this article further explains that in order to comply with the principle of proportionality, an "attack must be directed against a military objective with means which are not disproportionate in relation to the objective, but are suited to destroying only that objective, and the effects of the attacks must be limited in the way required by the Protocol; 'moreover,' even after those conditions are fulfilled, the incidental civilian losses and damages must not be excessive."[46]

It is with these principles in mind that one must analyze the evacuation of Aleppo, for it was done as a military operation in a time of armed conflict. One must ask several questions: Was the evacuation militarily necessary? Was the evacuation proportional to the concrete and direct military advantage gained? And, did these evacuations cause unnecessary human suffering that was not essential to the destruction of the enemy?

Although sieges are not *per se* a violation of international law, intentional starvation has been prohibited by Additional Protocol II.[47] There are numerous reports by human rights groups, including the VDC and even the UN report cited above that point to intentional starvation of both armed rebel groups and civilians in eastern Aleppo where the Syrian government's intention is to force the movement of both groups.

ADDITIONAL PROTOCOL II— ARTICLE 17

Article 17 of the Geneva Convention's Additional Protocol II prohibits the forced movement of civilians in times of non-international armed conflict.[48] This prohibition is a key element in the bulwark of civilian protection.

> 1. The displacement of the civilian population shall not be ordered for reasons related to the conflict unless the security of the civilians involved or imperative military reasons so demand. Should such displacements have to be carried out, all possible measures shall be taken in order that the civilian population may be received under satisfactory conditions of shelter, hygiene, health, safety and nutrition.
> 2. Civilians shall not be compelled to leave their own territory for reasons connected with the conflict.[49]

The issue of forced displacements was addressed in Article 49 of the Fourth Convention.[50] Article 49 covers instances of deportations, transfers, and evacuations from occupied territories. However, it does not protect in circumstances that fall within non-international armed conflicts like the one we see currently in Syria. Moreover, Common Article 3 of the Geneva Conventions does not address the issues of forced evacuations and displacements. Therefore, we see these issues addressed in Additional Protocol II.

The language of Article 17 was based on the wording of Article 49 of the Fourth Convention. Paragraph one of Article 17 applies to the displacement of civilians, whether in groups or individually, within the territory of a Contracting Party. While Syria has not signed nor ratified Additional Protocol II, it has since become customary international law.[51] It should also be noted that Article 17 does not restrict the freedom of civilians to move throughout the territory of the contracting party. Therefore, it is necessary to show that the displacement of civilians is indeed forced, and done against the will of those being displaced.

There are two categories of exceptions to the forced displacement of civilians. The first is in regards to the security of the civilian population. The second exception is for imperative military reasons. As the commentary remarks, any argument made regarding the military necessity of forced displacements will require a detailed assessment of the circumstances.[52]

The first exception to the rule is in cases that demand the displacement or evacuation of civilians for the sake of safety. This exception should be granted in cases where the circumstances lend to the conclusion that if not removed from a specific area the civilian population will be exposed to grave danger.

The second exception should be scrutinized and only be allowed when the military necessity is imperative. Political motives and justifications should never be used to displace civilians.[53] Therefore, unless to avoid grave danger, epidemics, or natural disasters, forcibly displacing civilians is a violation of Article 17.

Furthermore, paragraph one of Article 17 imposes a duty to provide shelter, hygiene, health, safety, and nutrition to those displaced civilians while being moved and where they will be received.[54] This duty ensures that even if a civilian population is displaced, necessities will be provided.

UNIVERSAL DECLARATION OF HUMAN RIGHTS

The Universal Declaration of Human Rights (UDHR)[55] has proven to be the "foundation of much of the post-1945 codification of human rights."[56] The Syrian Arab Republic voted in favor of the UDHR in 1948.[57] Among the efforts to "reaffirm faith in fundamental human rights,"[58] the UDHR outlines several rights that must be respected by all States. Among them is the right to "life, liberty, and security of person,"[59] the right to be free from arbitrary "arrest, detention, or exile,"[60] the right to "freedom of movement and residence within the borders of each state,"[61] as well as the right to "own property alone as well as in association with others"[62] and to not be arbitrarily deprived of his property.[63]

INTERNATIONAL COVENANT ON
CIVIL AND POLITICAL RIGHTS

The Syrian Arab Republic accessioned to the International covenant on Civil and Political Rights[64] (ICCPR) on April 21, 1969, and has therefore undertaken the recognition of the inherent dignity and the equal and inalienable rights of all members of the human family.[65] Among the rights specifically detailed in this Covenant, is the right of freedom of movement.[66] As the UN Human Rights Committee notes in General Comment No. 27, this right is an "indispensable condition for the free development of a person."[67] Moreover, the right to reside in a place of one's choice must also include the obligation to refrain from any form of forced displacement.[68]

There are instances where a set of circumstances exist that force the hand of a government to derogate from one or more rights set forth in the ICCPR.[69] This hedging may seem like an easy excuse from states. However, it provides for derogation under very specific situations—as well as a short amount of time for the state to act this way.[70] For example, during armed conflict—whether international or non-international—the rules of international humanitarian law become applicable and help to inform a state's emergency powers.[71] Among the fundamental requirements for any measure that derogates from the ICCPR is that it must be "strictly required by the exigencies of the situation."[72] This does not apply in the Syria context. There was a siege imposed upon eastern Aleppo by the Syrian government that lasted over 100 days. At any point in time the regime could have allowed for voluntary evacuation with proper documentation to ensure that no loss of property was realized.

INTERNATIONAL COVENANT ON ECONOMIC, SOCIAL, AND CULTURAL RIGHTS

The Syrian government has also accessioned to the International Covenant on Economic, Social, and Cultural Rights.[73] Article 11 of the ICESCR describes the obligation of states parties to the covenant to recognize and respect the right of "everyone to an adequate standard of living for himself and his family, including adequate food, clothing and housing, and to the continuous improvement of living conditions."[74] The Committee, in General Comment No. 4 (1991), observed that forced evictions are "*prima facie* incompatible with the requirements of the [ICESCR]."[75] Surely, unprovoked evictions are "gross violation[s] of human rights,"[76] but the question of when derogations may be acceptable remains. Recognizing that many instances of forced eviction are associated with violence, such as those resulting from armed conflict,[77] both the ICESCR and other legal instruments direct states parties to ensure all feasible alternatives have been explored, and avoid or minimize the need for the use of force.[78] General Comment No. 7 provides a list of procedural protections suggested for application in relation to these situations:

  a. an opportunity for genuine consultation with those affected;

b. adequate and reasonable notice for all affected persons prior to the scheduled date of eviction;
c. information on the proposed evictions, and, where applicable, on the alternative purpose for which the land or housing is to be used, to be made available in reasonable time to all those affected;
d. especially where groups of people are involved, government officials or their representatives to be present during an eviction;
e. all persons carrying out the eviction to be properly identified;
f. evictions not to take place in particularly bad weather or at night unless the affected persons consent otherwise;
g. provision of legal remedies; and
h. provision, where possible, of legal aid to persons who are in need of it to seek redress from the courts.[79]

Furthermore, if eviction is unavoidable, states parties must take any and all appropriate measures to ensure that alternative housing can be found.[80]

The situations in Darayya and Aleppo are clear violations of the ICESCR. There was no genuine consultation with the citizens of eastern Aleppo, only an order to evacuate or be destroyed. There were no minimization considerations. Furthermore, there has been little to no attempt to ensure evacuees are being provided with adequate housing following their evacuation.

CONCLUSION

The conflict in Syria has violated numerous international norms. This bloody and shattered end to the Arab Spring has now turned into the Arab Maelstrom. The conflict is emblematic to the new type of conflict of the twenty-first century, dirty little wars set in kaleidoscopic settings with a confused beginning and no rational end. The united national standard of restoring international peace and security is challenged. We now face conflict and unrest in regions of the world where restoration of a conflict may not be possible. Is the United Nations paradigm challenged as a result? Can the world live with only managing peace and security in various settings, beyond the ability and scope of the international community to completely restore a peace? This remains to be seen.

Civilians are and will continue to be caught up in these kaleidoscopic events and suffer the consequences as the conflicting parties step away from international norms and the laws of armed conflict. No more has this consequence been more apparent than in Syria over the past several years. The cornerstone principle of the laws of armed conflict that civilians cannot be intentionally attacked is simply ignored with the horrific consequences that we see today. Forcing civilian movement against their will for no apparent legal reason is simply wrong and illegal. At a minimum the party doing or supporting this type of action is committing serious violations of humanitarian law. In time it will be held accountable.

NOTES

David M. Crane would like to thank his two faculty assistants Casey Kooring and Andrew Dieselman for their extensive and helpful work on this project.

1. Al-Jazeera, Syria's Civil War Explained, Al-Jazeera (February 7, 2017), http://www.aljazeera.com/news/2016/05/syria-civil-war-explained-160505084119966.html; Lucy Rodgers, David Gritten, James Offer, and Patrick Asare, Syria: The Story of the Conflict, BBC (March 11, 2016), http://www.bbc.com/news/world-middle-east-26116868.

2. Who's Who in the Syrian Civil War, The Clarion Project (http://www.clarionproject.org/sites/default/files/Clarion%20Project%20Syrian%20Civil%20War%20Factsheet.pdf).

3. Common Article 2 of the Geneva Convention, 1949.

4. ICTY, *The Prosecutor v. Fatmir Limaj*, Judgment, IT-03- 66-T, November 30, 2005, para. 135–170.

5. See D. Schindler, The Different Types of Armed Conflicts According to the Geneva Conventions and Protocols, RCADI, Vol. 163, 1979-II, 147.

6. Additional Protocol II, art. 1, para. 1.

7. https://documents-dds-ny.un.org/doc/UNDOC/GEN/G17/026/63/PDF/G1702663.pdf?OpenElement 21.

8. https://documents-dds-ny.un.org/doc/UNDOC/GEN/G17/026/63/PDF/G1702663.pdf?OpenElement, 21.

9. https://documents-dds-ny.un.org/doc/UNDOC/GEN/G17/026/63/PDF/G1702663.pdf?OpenElement, 22 "three years of military impasse…"

10. https://documents-dds-ny.un.org/doc/UNDOC/GEN/G17/026/63/PDF/G1702663.pdf?OpenElement, 22.

11. https://documents-dds-ny.un.org/doc/UNDOC/GEN/G17/026/63/PDF/G1702663.pdf?OpenElement, 22.

12. https://documents-dds-ny.un.org/doc/UNDOC/GEN/G17/026/63/PDF/G1702663.pdf?OpenElement, 23. The Ba'ath Brigades, the Tiger Forces, and the Liwa al-Quds Brigade of Syria as well as the Army of the Guardians of the Islamic Revolution al-Quds Force, Hizbullah, Afghan militias and the Iraqi al-Nujabaa and al-Fatimiyoon militias.

13. Special Report on the Evacuation of Civilians from East Aleppo, Violations Documentation Center in Syria, 2017, http://vdc-sy.net/Website/wp-content/uploads/2017/01/Aleppo-report-En-.pdf.

14. Ibid.

15. Ibid.

16. Ibid. This effectively ended the 112-day siege on eastern Aleppo.

17. Ibid., 7.

18. Ibid., 12.

19. Al Jazeera, Syria: Evacuation of Daraya Begins in deal to end siege, Al Jazeera (August 27, 2016), http://www.aljazeera.com/news/2016/08/syria-aid-convoys-enter-daraya-deal-siege-160826084006363.html.

20. Merrit Kennedy, After 4 Years Of Siege, Civilians and Rebels Evacuate Syria's Daraya, NPR (August 26, 2016), http://www.npr.org/sections/thetwo-way/2016/08/26/491474426/after-4-years-of-siege-civilians-and-rebels-evacuate-syrias-daraya.

21. Alice Fordham, Syrian Government in Control After Rebels Evacuate Daraya, NPR (August 29, 2016), http://www.npr.org/2016/08/29/491770330/syrian-government-in-control-after-rebels-evacuate-daraya.

22. Ibid.

23. Ibid.

24. Merrit Kennedy, After 4 Years Of Siege, Civilians and Rebels Evacuate Syria's Daraya, NPR (August 26, 2016), http://www.npr.org/sections/thetwo-way/2016/08/26/491474426/after-4-years-of-siege-civilians-and-rebels-evacuate-syrias-daraya.

25. Alice Fordham, Syrian Government in Control After Rebels Evacuate Daraya, NPR (August 29, 2016), http://www.npr.org/2016/08/29/491770330/syrian-government-in-control-after-rebels-evacuate-daraya.

26. Ibid.

27. Ibid.

28. Alice Fordham, The Siege That Keeps a Rebel Town in Syrian Desperate for Food Aid, NPR (July 12, 2016), http://www.npr.org/sections/parallels/2016/07/12/484946410/the-siege-that-keeps-a-rebel-town-in-syria-desperate-for-food-aid.

29. Ibid.

30. Ibid.

31. Merrit Kennedy, After 4 Years Of Siege, Civilians and Rebels Evacuate Syria's Daraya, NPR (August 26, 2016), http://www.npr.org/sections/thetwo-way/2016/08/26/491474426/after-4-years-of-siege-civilians-and-rebels-evacuate-syrias-daraya.

32. Alice Fordham, Syrian Government in Control After Rebels Evacuate Daraya, NPR (August 29, 2016), http://www.npr.org/2016/08/29/491770330/syrian-government-in-control-after-rebels-evacuate-daraya.

33. Merrit Kennedy, After 4 Years Of Siege, Civilians and Rebels Evacuate Syria's Daraya, NPR (August 26, 2016), http://www.npr.org/sections/thetwo-way/2016/08/26/491474426/after-4-years-of-siege-civilians-and-rebels-evacuate-syrias-daraya.

34. Ibid.

35. Amanda Alexander, *A Short History of International Humanitarian Law*, 26 Eur. J. Int'l L. 109 (2015).

36. International Committee of the Red Cross (ICRC), *War and International Humanitarian Law* (October 29, 2010), available at www.icrc.org/eng/war-and-law/overview-war-and-law.htm (last visited December 20, 2014).

37. L. Oppenheim, *International Law: A Treatise,* edited by R. F. Roxburgh (3rd edn, 1921).

38. Ibid. at 227. (Oppenheim describes this principle as the idea that "a belligerent is justified in applying any amount and any kind of force which is necessary for the realization of the purpose of war—namely, the overpowering of the opponent.")

39. Hague Convention, preamble.

40. Oppenheim, *supra* n. 4.

41. Alexander, *supra* n. 2.

42. Shindler & Toman, at 650.

43. Ibid.

44. Art. 50, para. 1. Art. 4, in part, states: "A. Prisoners of war. . . are persons belonging to one of the following categories, who have fallen into the power of the enemy: (1) Members of the armed forces of a Party to the conflict as well as members of militias or volunteer corps forming part of such armed forces. (2) Members of other militias and members of other volunteer corps, including those of organized resistance movements, belonging to a Party to the conflict and operating in or outside their own territory, even if this territory is occupied, provided that such militias or volunteer corps, including such organized resistance movements, fulfill the following conditions: (a) that of being commanded by a person responsible for his subordinates; (b) that of having a fixed distinctive sign recognizable at a distance; (c) that of carrying arms openly; (d) that of conducting their operations in accordance with the laws and customs of war. (3) Members of regular armed forces who profess allegiance to a government or an authority not recognized by the Detaining Power . . . (6) Inhabitants of a non-occupied territory, who on the approach of the enemy spontaneously take up arms to resist the invading forces, without having had time to form themselves into regular armed units, provided they carry arms openly and respect the laws and customs of war." *See generally* Parks, *Air War and the Law of War*, Air Force Law Review 1, beginning at 111 (1990).

45. API, art. 51(b).

46. Commentary, para. 1979.

47. Additional Protocol II to the Geneva Conventions of 12 August 1949, and Relating to the Protection of Victims of Non-International Armed Conflict, Art. 14, June 8, 1977 (http://www.redcross.org/images/MEDIA_CustomProductCatalog/m27740272_Additional_Protocol_II.pdf).

48. Additional Protocol II, Art. 17, Para. 1 and 2. (http://www.loc.gov/rr/frd/Military_Law/pdf/Commentary_GC_Protocols.pdf).

49. Additional Protocol II, Art. 17 (http://www.loc.gov/rr/frd/Military_Law/pdf/Commentary_GC_Protocols.pdf).

50. See Geneva Convention Relative to the Protection of Civilians in Time of War, Art. 49, Aug. 12, 1949 (https://ihl-databases.icrc.org/ihl/WebART/380-600056).

51. International Committee of the Red Cross, Study on Customary International Humanitarian Law: Rule 129. The Act of Displacement (2017), https://ihl-databases.icrc.org/customary-ihl/eng/docs/v1_rul_rule129.

52. Additional Protocol II, Art. 17, Commentary Para. 4853

53. Ibid. at Para. 4854

54. Ibid. at Para. 4856

55. Universal Declaration of Human Rights [hereafter UDHR], G.A. Res. 217, U.N. GAOR, 3d Sess., U.N. Doc A/810 (1948).

56. Hurst Hannum, *The Status of the Universal Declaration of Human Rights in National and International Law*, 25 Ga. J. Int'l & Comp. L. 287, 289 (1995/96).

57. UN Voting Record of the Universal Declaration of Human Rights, United Nations Bibliographic Information System (0ADAD), (http://unbisnet.un.org:8080/ipac20/ipac.jsp?session=132G11114932H.82867&profile=voting&uri=full=3100023~!909326~!0&ri=7&aspect=power&menu=search&source=~!horizon (last visited Mar 9, 2017).

58. Preamble of UN Charter.

59. UDHR, Art. 3.

60. UDHR, Art. 9.

61. UDHR, Art. 13(1).

62. UDHR, Art. 17(1).

63. UDHR, Art. 17(2).

64. UN General Assembly, *International Covenant on Civil and Political Rights* [hereafter ICCPR], December 16, 1966, United Nations, Treaty Series, vol. 999, p. 171, available at: http://www.refworld.org/docid/3ae6b3aa0.html (accessed February 24, 2017).

65. Preamble of ICCPR.

66. ICCPR, Art. 12.

67. UN Human Rights Committee (HRC), *CCPR General Comment No. 27: Article 12 (Freedom of Movement)*, 1, 2 November 1999, CCPR/C/21/Rev.1/Add.9, available at: http://www.refworld.org/docid/45139c394.html (accessed February 24, 2017).

68. UN Human Rights Committee (HRC), *CCPR General Comment No. 27: Article 12 (Freedom of Movement)*, ¶7, 2 November 1999, CCPR/C/21/Rev.1/Add.9, available at: http://www.refworld.org/docid/45139c394.html [accessed February 24, 2017].

69. ICCPR, Art. 4.

Article 4

1. In time of public emergency which threatens the life of the nation and the existence of which is officially proclaimed, the States Parties to the present Covenant may take measures derogating from their obligations under the present Covenant to the extent strictly required by the exigencies of the situation, provided that such measures are not inconsistent with their other obligations under international law and do not involve discrimination solely on the ground of race, colour, sex, language, religion or social origin.

2. No derogation from articles 6, 7, 8 (paragraphs I and 2), 11, 15, 16 and 18 may be made under this provision.

3. Any State Party to the present Covenant availing itself of the right of derogation shall immediately inform the other States Parties to the present Covenant, through the intermediary of the Secretary-General of the United Nations, of the provisions

from which it has derogated and of the reasons by which it was actuated. A further communication shall be made, through the same intermediary, on the date on which it terminates such derogation.

70. *See* UN Human Rights Committee (HRC), *CCPR General Comment No. 29: Article 4: Derogations during a State of Emergency*, 1–2, 31 August 2001, CCPR/C/21/Rev.1/Add.11, available at: http://www.refworld.org/docid/453883fd1f.html (accessed 24 February 2017).

71. Explored above.

72. UN Human Rights Committee (HRC), *CCPR General Comment No. 29: Article 4: Derogations during a State of Emergency*, 4, August 31, 2001, CCPR/C/21/Rev.1/Add.11, available at: http://www.refworld.org/docid/453883fd1f.html (accessed February 24, 2017). ("This requirement relates to the duration, geographical coverage and material scope of the state of emergency and any measures of derogation resorted to because of the emergency.")

73. *International Covenant on Economic, Social, and Cultural Rights* [hereafter ICESCR], New York, 16 December 1966, *United Nations Treaty Series*, vol. 993, p. 3, available from: www.???.un.org. Syria accessioned on April 21, 1969.

74. ICESCR, art. 11(1).

75. UN Committee on Economic, Social and Cultural Rights (CESCR), *General Comment No. 7: The right to adequate housing (Art.11.1): forced evictions*, 1, May 20, 1997, E/1998/22, available at: http://www.refworld.org/docid/47a70799d.html, *citing* UN Committee on Economic, Social and Cultural Rights (CESCR), *General Comment No. 4: The Right to Adequate Housing (Art. 11 (1) of the Covenant)*, 13, 13 December 1991, E/1992/23, available at: http://www.refworld.org/docid/47a7079a1.html (accessed February 24, 2017).

76. Commission on Human Rights resolution 1993/77, 1.

77. UN Committee on Economic, Social and Cultural Rights (CESCR), *General Comment No. 7: The right to adequate housing (Art.11.1): forced evictions*, 6, May 20, 1997, E/1998/22, available at: http://www.refworld.org/docid/47a70799d.html.

78. UN Committee on Economic, Social and Cultural Rights (CESCR), *General Comment No. 7: The right to adequate housing (Art.11.1): forced evictions*, 13, May 20, 1997, E/1998/22, available at: http://www.refworld.org/docid/47a70799d.html.

79. UN Committee on Economic, Social and Cultural Rights (CESCR), *General Comment No. 7: The right to adequate housing (Art.11.1): forced evictions*, 15, May 20, 1997, E/1998/22, available at: http://www.refworld.org/docid/47a70799d.html.

80. UN Committee on Economic, Social and Cultural Rights (CESCR), *General Comment No. 7: The right to adequate housing (Art.11.1): forced evictions*, 16, May 20, 1997, E/1998/22, available at: http://www.refworld.org/docid/47a70799d.html.

Chapter Four

Stories from the Hill

Sarajevo and Darayya

Janine di Giovanni with Sophia Slater

Despite the endless diplomatic dithering, the broken ceasefires, the days and weeks spent waiting for air strikes, there was the belief that hope was slowly filtering out of the place as the West refused to act. [1]

I wrote these words in 1994, reflecting on my time living intermittently in Sarajevo during the siege from 1992–1996. Wandering amongst the destroyed neighborhoods, visiting my friends who were existing on humanitarian aid rations of food—rice, flour, some packages of shapeless, colorless food—I wrote down as much as I could in my growing collection of notebooks. My goal during this period of my life was to not forget, to remember what the days of the siege were like, how people lived, how they died. I believed that after seeing humanity reach such a point of desperation, it would not happen again in my lifetime. Or at least, I would not witness it.

I was wrong.

The Siege of Sarajevo began on April 6, 1992, after Serb militants started indiscriminately shooting the thousands of peaceful protestors who had gathered in Sarajevo following sectarian violence the previous day. It would go on for more than three years, until the Bosnian government finally declared its end on February 29, 1996. The violent three-year siege is now recognized as the longest siege of any country's capital city in the history of modern warfare. With over 11,000 casualties, it lasted three years, ten months, three weeks, and three days. I remember the day that I heard the tram bells ringing—for years the trams had been silenced as they ran down the center of the city's "Sniper's Alley." My friends always told me that the day they heard the bells meant it would be the end of the siege, and life would return to normal. Or, as normal as it could be for people who had lived under medieval conditions for so long.

Over 20 years later, I am watching in horror as the civilian toll in Syria continues to rise, the highly organized and deadly activities of radical Islamic terrorist groups wreaking havoc in a region that has long been destabilized. As I sit down to write this, it is disheartening that those words I wrote so many years ago about Sarajevo also applied to Darayya, a city that also endured a brutal siege, as long as Sarajevo's, until October 2016.

I have not forgotten about Sarajevo, and I believe it is now worth examining the Siege of Darayya in this context, looking at historical cycles that are reoccurring in different ways. This also serves as a larger examination of how sieges function, and how entire communities come to be held hostage. At the same time, from a journalistic perspective this is a difficult examination to conduct. After Bosnia, many of us in the journalistic community said "never again." I was sure that the world would never again watch in silence as hundreds of thousands of people were systematically starved, beaten, bombed, traumatized, and denied the most basic human rights, such as education and medical care. The civil war in Syria today shows me I was deeply mistaken.

The Siege of Darayya began on November 9, 2012, instigated by the Syrian Armed Forces—fighting on behalf of Bashar al-Assad's government—after various rebel groups had established their presence in Darayya and Muadamiyat al-Sham, suburbs of the Syrian capital of Damascus. Both Darayya and Muadamiyat al-Sham were put under siege, with nearly continuous airstrikes launched by the Syrian Air Force for the next nearly four years. After much negotiation, on August 24, 2016, the Syrian Armed Forces agreed to end the siege on the condition that the rebels would abandon the areas of Darayya under their control.

On October 19 of the same year, the siege of Muadamiyat al-Sham was also broken, again under the condition that rebel groups evacuate the area. While the exact number of casualties is unknown, over 160,000 people were internally displaced in the siege. The dual siege of Darayya and Muadamiyat al-Sham would not be over for three years, eleven months, one week, and three days.

The basic military tactics of a siege have largely remained the same, as have the methods of psychological warfare. In Sarajevo, a psychiatrist friend once told me the entire city at one point during the siege was a "walking insane asylum" due to the number of people who were deeply and permanently traumatized.

This seemed logical to me. The city had become apocalyptic with packs of wild dogs running through the streets, blood stains on the bomb-scarred roads, and children dying simply because they went outside to play. At the core of the mentality of those who take cities hostage is the desire to wear down the civilian population, with the intent of making those civilians believe they are paying a steep price for "supporting" the opposition—never mind that people mostly end up desperately wanting to survive and feed their families as opposed to having an ideological shift in how they view the opposition. In order to effectively punish the civilians for not supporting a certain powerful group, community institutions such as schools and hospitals, for example, were targeted by airstrikes in both Sarajevo and Darayya.

Hospitals are always easy targets, with sick people and doctors somehow portrayed as the enemy. On the night of August 19, 2016, barrel bombs were dropped on a medical facility in Darayya, the only remaining hospital that had served the 8,000 civilians left in the city. The Syrian Armed Forces were widely blamed for the attack, and Human Rights Watch quickly condemned the Syrian government's widespread use of incendiary weapons.[2]

My memories of Sarajevo are similar. Dr. Vesna Cegnic, a surgeon whom I met when she was working at the State Hospital in Sarajevo, did not know whether she would be able to continue providing medical care from one day to the next. Her hospital was constantly bombed, and she had to administer medicine and try to save lives in nearly medieval conditions. Perhaps the bombs have become more sophisticated and deadly over the past 20+ years, but the intent is the same: the fewer hospitals there are, the more people will suffer.

There were some days in Bosnia where it seemed the war would drag on forever, with both the Bosnian government and foreign powers seemingly stalled. I had hoped that diplomatic negotiations would become more effective with time, and that the international community would have learned that swift and decisive action is needed when a city is under siege. By the time NATO had begun posing ultimatums in Bosnia in 1994, Sarajevo had already been under siege for two years. While the Serbs did grudgingly roll back their military presence in the hills above Sarajevo, it would be almost two more years until the siege was declared over. I saw firsthand the daily horrors of that siege, so it is almost unfathomable that there were no effective punitive measures imposed by the international community to break the siege in Darayya.

What were we doing for four years? How did we effectively sit and watch while Syrians suffered unimaginable atrocities using incendiary weapons and other tactics that are blatantly in violation of international law? By "we," I mean the American government, the British government, the French government. I also mean "we" the people in those countries. There were certain individuals across these groups of people who made efforts to intervene in the worsening Syrian Civil War, but simply put the people of Darayya, and Syria, in general, seemed not to be enough of a priority.

Seeking to end the conflict, former US Secretary of State John Kerry had endless negotiations with his Russian counterpart Sergei V. Lavrov, failing time and time again to establish a ceasefire that would hold. Meanwhile, the Obama administration focused almost exclusively on military action that was considered anti-terrorist as opposed to humanitarian support, deciding that helping to alleviate the suffering of the Syrian people was not worth engaging in another bloody Middle East conflict. The US supported various non-governmental groups, but could not negotiate an outright stop to the violence.

By the end of 2016, the US was cut out of peace talks entirely when only Russia, Iran, and Turkey met to discuss the future of Syria.[3] While there were occasional ceasefires, the talks were largely a failure for Kerry and the US.

Staffan di Mistura, the UN Special Envoy to Syria, also failed despite extraordinary efforts to convince both sides in the Syrian war to end their attacks. By 2017, the new Trump presidency could barely muster representation at the Astana talks on Syria, and when the Geneva IV talks were launched in February of this year, they seemed doomed to fail from the beginning. Too little, too late.

It is important to note that during these extensive deliberations, President al-Assad has continued his military attacks in Syria, with Russia's military and strategic support. It is thus the Syrian civilians who suffered most while the international community was going in circles. Even in Darayya, after almost four years, it was an agreement between al-Assad's regime and the rebels that ended the siege, with little to no diplomatic pressure from the international community.

The end of the Siege of Sarajevo precipitated differently, with the Dayton Accords signed by then-President of the Republic of Serbia Slobodan Milosevic representing Bosnian Serbs, then-President of Croatia Franjo Tudman, and then-President of Bosnia and Herzegovina Alija Izetbegovic. This treaty was facilitated by then-US Secretary of State Warren Christopher, with others representing the EU, Russia, and the UK. While the goal of the treaty was to immediately halt the military conflict in Bosnia, it was also fairly flexible, allowing for a true rebuilding of the region.

Dayton was not without flaws, specifically concerning the ethno-religious factions that existed in the former Yugoslavia. On numerous trips back to the region, post-war, I continued to see shards of the hatred and bitterness and I never had the sense that reconciliation had occurred on that air strip in Dayton, Ohio. The various parties had effectively been bullied into ending the war by the US, and the treaty was a military one more than anything else, not hugely concerned with bridging cultural differences. But it worked: the agreement was ratified in late 1995, and by early spring of 1996 the siege of Sarajevo was broken. There is at least a chance of overcoming religious and cultural divisions, however deep, when people are not being blown to pieces left and right.

Looking back at Bosnia, the war in Syria is infinitely more complex given the existence of the Islamic State (IS), the Sunni extremist terrorist organization also known as ISIS, ISIL, or Daesh. IS has a stronghold on the area surrounding the Syrian city of Raqqa, to the country's northeast. As reporters on the ground, we first became aware of their existence in 2012. While the US had been involved on some level in supporting select non-IS rebel groups since the war first broke out, it was not until IS overran Mosul in June, 2014 that Washington sat up in horror, blindsided by this terrorist organization that seemingly came out of nowhere. The US only had to look at their handling of the Iraqi occupation following the fall of Saddam Hussein to get those answers.

Given the prevalence of IS in Iraq and Syria, many foreign countries have stated as their objective the elimination of the group as opposed to a military campaign against the policies and tactics of President al-Assad. President Donald Trump continued this line of rhetoric, his key message being that there are two directly opposing sides: the "good guys" (Russia, US, and President Assad); and the "bad guys" (IS). In my view, this oversimplification has been dangerous, allowing governments to hide behind their focus on terrorism while neglecting the millions of civilians who are suffering.

The US coalition, including the UK and France, has been accused of indirectly funding IS in their support of rebel groups in Syria, making it geopolitically imperative that the American side emphasizes its focus on defeating IS. Russian President Vladimir Putin, on the other hand, in a highly performative show of his supposed intent to take down IS, has decided to side with the Syrian regime. In light of this balancing act that non-Middle Eastern powers are trying to maintain, intervention in situations such as the Siege of Darayya, where the Syrian regime was accused of much of the violence against the civilians, was never as much of a priority for Western countries involved in the region.

Another significant difference between Sarajevo and Darayya is the degree to which foreign journalists and human rights monitors have been allowed access, thereby recording the suffering and bringing it to the public in real time. In Sarajevo, as journalists we were allowed to go to the frontlines or travel with soldiers as long as each of us took responsibility for our own life. This kept the tragedies unfolding in Sarajevo and the rest of Bosnia consistently at the forefront of public awareness, forcing world leaders such as then-British Prime Minister Margaret Thatcher to take a stand on the conflict there.

In Syria, travel is heavily restricted by the government. The only options are either to get a visa from the al-Assad regime as a "friendly" journalist, meaning one who has written favorably about the regime, or to cross into the country illegally. The borders from Turkey and Lebanon are dangerous and nearly impossible to cross. Attempts to take this route into Syria often result in kidnapping and murder, as seen in the tragic deaths of Americans Steven Sotloff and James Foley, both of whom were beheaded by IS.

It is extremely difficult as a foreign reporter to get into Syria let alone to the frontlines. Aid convoys from the UN and other humanitarian organizations have frequently been blocked from entering cities under siege, whether it be Darayya or Aleppo, and there are not reliable statistics for the number of casualties in Syria due to conflicting reports and almost no independent witnesses. The UN has no permanent presence in the region and does not track casualties in Syria anymore, as conflict areas are tightly locked down and verification of reports that do come out is close to impossible.[4] Despite our current digital age of social media, information coming out of Syria is severely limited.

This is a far cry from the UN International Police Task Force (IPTF) and UN civilian office created in Bosnia and Herzegovina to monitor and report on the conditions there. These offices were established in 1995, three years after the initial conflict broke out. The Syrian Civil War is in its sixth year. That said, I distinctly recall then-UN Secretary General Boutros-Boutros Ghali coming to Sarajevo and blithely stating that there were ten places in the world that were worse off than the Bosnian capital. Foreign support wouldn't come for years. The international community has been failing the civilians of conflict zones for decades

Throughout these various differences, the hardships and unending resilience of people under siege remains remarkably constant. While watching the horrors of siege in Darayya these past few years or in Sarajevo in the early 1990s, it is easy to forget that for the people actually surviving the siege, while the physical destruction is terrifying and dangerous, it is still profoundly painful to lose the mundane things of their everyday life: food that is not from a humanitarian package; a football game watched on television while relaxing with family; a swim in the Mijalcka River, which runs through Sarajevo, on a gentle summer day.

A woman in Syria told me the thing she missed the most was watching her fruit trees bloom, and being able to go outside to pick peaches and apples without being blown to shreds. It is the little things, those with emotional value, that people miss the most, as those were the things that still remind them of their humanity. This longing is what wore down people's souls during both sieges.

One afternoon, at the height of the Siege of Darayya, a friend of mine named Mohammed texted me to see if I could send him articles I had written while in besieged Sarajevo. "So we can understand how the Bosnian people survived," he explained, "and we can learn from them." I realized that my friends from Sarajevo were some of the most resilient people I had met in my life. I thought they could maybe offer some advice, as siege survivors, to the people in Darayya still living through the siege. "Does he want to know how to make oil lamps or how to stop going insane?" asked Aida Cerkez, who had lived through the Siege of Sarajevo and was now an AP reporter there. "I mean, we can help him with both."

In the summer of 2016, I started the Sarajevo-Darayya group on WhatsApp. It included a sizeable group of people I knew from Sarajevo, all eager to help Mohammed through some of his darkest days. Zoran, a former Bosnian soldier, suggested playing cards. Nihad, who was a young boy during the Bosnian war, provided a list of films that he thought might offer Mohammed spiritual and emotional strength if he ever got electricity back to watch them. Samir, with whom I became very close friends in Sarajevo, said that maintaining humor was essential. We lost contact with Mohammed for a while, but he finally resurfaced in Idlib. I hope we played some small part in his survival.

Sarajevo today is functional again, but it will never be what it used to be for the people who lived there before, during, and after the siege. The siege may be over in Darayya, but its effects will be felt long after the brutality in Syria has subsided. In Darayya, as in Sarajevo, the exploding bombs, the snipers' bullets in civilians' spines and lungs, and the exhausted surgeons performing surgery in barely functional hospitals were all abhorrent. But perhaps the cruelest thing was the constant attempt to destroy the spirit. Sieges destroy the body, but far more permanently, they annihilate the soul.

NOTES

1. Di Giovanni, Janine. "The Quick and the Dead: Under Siege in Sarajevo." (1994), 2–3.

2. Human Rights Watch. "Time to Act against Incendiary Weapons." Human Rights Watch, December 12, 2016, www.hrw.org/news/2016/12/12/time-act-against-incendiary-weapons.

3. Hubbard, Ben, and David E. Sanger. "Russia, Iran and Turkey Meet for Syria Talks, Excluding U.S." *New York Times*, December 21, 2016, www.nytimes.com/2016/12/20/world/middleeast/russia-iran-and-turkey-meet-for-syria-talks-excluding-us.html.

4. BBC. "Islamic State and the Crisis in Iraq and Syria in Maps." BBC News, March 28, 2018, www.bbc.com/news/world-middle-east-27838034.

Chapter Five

Syria's Green Buses, "Evacuation Deals," and Forced Displacement

Mai El-Sadany

As the Chinese-made, 2009-model, lime-green buses[1] that once transported students to school and workers to their places of employment arrive,[2] men, women, and children who have been bombarded with barrel bombs, placed under siege for years, and brought to the point of starvation, begin to say goodbye to the homes that they have lived in their entire lives. In the weeks just prior, they had been the recipients of leaflets and fliers offering them a "choice" between departure and death.[3] They prepare to embark on a journey that will either take them to a government-controlled area where opposition fighters and individuals perceived to be in opposition to the government risk interrogation, forced conscription, or arrest, or to an area outside of government-control that is likely to soon become the site of airstrikes, bombardment, and sieges yet again.[4] This journey not only displaces them from their properties, their histories, and their heritage, but is the final stage in a concerted policy by Bashar al-Assad's regime to consolidate territory, expel citizens who are not loyal to the Syrian president, and make lasting changes to the country's political and sectarian demographics.

"COORDINATED AND PLANNED"

Throughout the war, Syrian government forces and their allies targeted numerous opposition-controlled areas in this manner, employing what popularly became known as "surrender or starve" campaigns. Per these campaigns, entry and exit points into a target area would first be sealed by government and allied forces; civilians who would attempt to leave the target area would be prevented from doing so, arrested, or shot at. As time would pass, food, water, medicine, and fuel would begin to dwindle; supply and humanitarian aid convoys would be prevented from entering the city. At the same time, barrel bombs and airstrikes would begin to bombard the area, leading to the death of civilians and rescue workers, the targeting of hospitals and civil defense centers, and the terrorizing of the population. Ill or injured civilians would not be allowed to evacuate the city for treatment. Children, women, and men would begin to suffer and possibly die of malnutrition, infectious diseases, and bombing injuries.[5] After months, if not years, of sustained siege, those managing the area would be left with no choice but to sign off on an "evacuation deal" that would result in the displacement of the area's residents from their homes.[6] Once the city had been emptied of its original inhabitants, it would—in many instances—then see its population replaced with government loyalists,[7] a move that would allow the Syrian regime to consolidate control over the area and more easily claim legitimacy.[8]

In legal terms, the "evacuation deals" that the Syrian regime militarily compelled upon its population constitute forced displacements. As will be demonstrated in the pages that follow, these evacuations were not one-off incidents, but rather, part of what the Independent International Commission of Inquiry on the Syrian Arab Republic has described as "coordinated and planned."[9] The commission has further underscored the political purpose behind these evacuations, noting: "Overall, the pattern of evacuations occurring countrywide appears intended to engineer changes to the political demographies of previously besieged enclaves, by redrawing and consolidating bases of political support."[10]

HOMS

One of the first cities to become the target of forced evacuations was Homs, an urban center whose people had taken to the streets to protest against the Syrian regime beginning on March 18, 2011. By early 2012, many of the residential non-Alawite neighborhoods of Homs had come under the control of opposition forces.[11]

In February 2012, the Syrian army launched a major military campaign against several opposition-controlled neighborhoods, among them Baba Amr. Subjected to intense bombardment and siege for about one month, Baba Amr was eventually forced to surrender, leading to the displacement of between 50,000 and 60,000 persons from the area alone. Fighting then continued across the rest of Homs, barrel bombs were used for the first time, and massacres by pro-government militias took place, forcing thousands of civilians to flee. By June 2012, government forces had forcibly depopulated a number of neighborhoods in Homs, many of them bordering pro-Assad, Alawite areas. In July 2012, Syrian government forces re-exerted their attention on a number of opposition-controlled neighborhoods, imposing sieges that involved access closures. By December 2012, Syrian government forces had regained control over most of Homs and by mid-2013, Hezbollah's capture of the neighboring Qusair further consolidated the siege of Homs. The city continued to witness decreasing levels of food, water, medicine, and fuel;[12] many civilians began showing signs of malnutrition and some resorted to eating leaves in order to survive.[13]

As the people of Homs were presented with the "choice" between surrender and death, a series of "evacuation deals" between February and May 2014 were reached; the Chinese green buses arrived to empty the besieged city, taking opposition fighters and the civilians who resided alongside them to al-Waer or the northern Homs countryside. Even as the displacement took place, hundreds of evacuated men were detained by the Syrian regime at checkpoints; some were arrested, others tortured, and some were even, killed.[14]

Ultimately, these "evacuation deals" resulted in the displacement of Homs's original residents and their replacement with regime loyalists and foreign settlers, contributing to a political and sectarian demographic shift in the population. After the evacuations took place, reports began to emerge that pro-government Shia and Alawite persons from the neighboring countryside had begun moving into Homs; they seized the homes of the city's former residents and gained permission from government officials to resettle and build new suburban houses.[15] Reports also surfaced that in some cases, a number of original residents who attempted to return to Homs were denied reentry into their homes; in those cases, Syrian regime officials would claim that these residents failed to provide sufficient proof that they used to reside there,[16] or that they needed to ascertain permission from local police stations to return. A report that interviewed displaced residents from Homs points to sectarian violence by pro-government militias, property record destruction, and the illegal resale of homes as additional factors that have furthered and continue to further the forced demographic changes in Homs and that have impeded and continue to impede the ability of its original residents to return.[17]

DARAYYA

Darayya, which became a symbol of nonviolent resistance against the brutality of the Syrian regime and the extremism of Al-Qaeda and the Islamic State, would also become the target of forced evacuations.

In light of its strategic proximity to the capital of Damascus and a neighboring military airport, Darayya was placed under siege by Syrian government forces. The full siege began in November 2012 and lasted about 1,368 days. During the siege, Darayya's citizens were deprived of regular access to food, water, and medical aid. June 2016 marked one of the only times that the city received food aid during its four-year siege; however, even as the aid was being delivered, Syrian government forces continued to bomb the city, making distributions remarkably difficult.

Describing the intense campaign targeting the people of Darayya, independent monitoring initiative Siege Watch wrote: "Darayya signaled the shift from the 'surrender or starve' campaigns of attrition to a much more aggressive 'surrender or die' approach aimed at quickly pushing besieged communities to the point of surrender and/or physical collapse."[18] Throughout the siege, at least 56 attacks on vital civilian facilities and eight chemical weapons attacks took place. Over 817 civilians were killed; six individuals died due to food shortages and three individuals died due to inadequate access to medicine.[19] Terrorized by heavy missile attacks, bombarded by over 9,000 barrel bombs throughout the siege,[20] and subjected to scorched-earth tactics that destroyed agricultural fields,[21] the population's opposition fighters and civilians—estimated to total around 5,000 persons at the time—were forced into an "evacuation deal" in August 2016 that displaced portions of the population to opposition-held Idlib and others to government-controlled suburbs.

Many of Darayya's original residents reportedly opted to go to Idlib out of a fear that they would be arrested, tortured, or killed for their participation in protests against the regime should they have relocated to government-controlled areas.[22] In fact, an Amnesty International report confirms that some of those displaced to the government-controlled suburbs of Damascus—many of them women and children—were arrested at checkpoints despite having undergone the necessary security screenings.[23]

Shortly after the forced evacuation of Darayya's original residents, Syrian government forces were reportedly seen looting homes and properties.[24] Additionally, at least 300 families belonging to the Shia Iraqi al-Nujaba Movement were reported to have arrived in Darayya after the evacuations[25], ushering in the beginning of yet another chapter in the regime's pursuit of political and sectarian demographic change. In a report published in September 2018, analyst Haid Haid confirms that Darayya's original residents have not been allowed to permanently return to Darayya and that the Syrian regime has installed a dozen checkpoints around the city to guarantee that this remains the case. Although some original residents have been allowed to make short-term visits, they have only been allowed to do so after undergoing a lengthy and involved security process that most cannot complete.[26]

EASTERN ALEPPO

Although the siege of opposition-held Eastern Aleppo would catch widespread and unprecedented international attention, its people too would face a similar fate to the residents of Homs and Darayya.

By the summer of 2012, most of the suburbs of Aleppo had come under the control of the Syrian opposition. In the months thereafter, opposition-held areas expanded to include eastern Aleppo. As the city came to be divided between a government-controlled western Aleppo and an opposition-run eastern Aleppo, Syrian and Russian government forces began to carry out attacks on civilians using cluster munitions, incendiary weapons, and air-delivered munitions on the eastern portion of the city. By August 2016, eastern Aleppo was brought under complete siege; more than 350,000 persons were besieged.

Despite a temporary gain by the Syrian opposition that broke the siege for a short period of time, government forces were able to impose yet another siege in September 2016, ultimately trapping about 250,000 individuals. In October 2016, Syrian government planes dropped leaflets over the besieged population that read: "If you do not leave this area immediately you will be finished. You know that everyone has given up on you. They left you alone to face your doom."[27] Hospitals, ambulances, schools, and residential areas were deliberately targeted; Syrian government forces, backed by their Russian allies, used internationally-prohibited cluster munitions, incendiary weapons, and chemicals on the civilian population.[28] Despite freezing temperatures and conditions, agencies were blocked from delivering assistance, including food and medicine. Humanitarian aid workers and citizen journalists were targeted by the government's strikes.[29]

Assad's intentions for eastern Aleppo were made explicitly clear; in the fall of 2016, he announced his intention to "cleanse" the city.[30] Conditions in the opposition-held eastern Aleppo became too difficult to bear throughout the end of 2016 and the risk of imminent mass starvation[31] came upon the population. In the last week of November 2016, Syrian government ground forces were able to split eastern Aleppo into two, and by mid-December, just five percent of eastern Aleppo remained in the hands of the opposition. Around this time, credible reports surfaced that pro-Assad forces, among them the Shia Iraqi al-Nujaba Movement, carried out summary executions of civilians.[32] Ultimately, the Violations Documentation Center recorded at least 3,497 civilian deaths during the offensive on eastern Aleppo (between June 2016 and mid-December 2016).[33]

After a forced "evacuation deal" was initially struck on December 13, various complications took place in the days that followed, from Iranian-backed militias halting a preliminary wave of Chinese green buses[34] to direct attacks on the convoys.[35] When a final "evacuation deal" was ultimately settled on, it involved reciprocal evacuations between eastern Aleppo, the besieged villages of Foua and Kefraya, and Zabadani and Madaya. Evacuations began more consistently on December 18 and by December 22, Syrian government forces announced that they had regained control over the entire city of Aleppo.[36]

Among those forcibly evacuated, some were sent to Idlib, while others were sent to western Aleppo and the western Aleppo countryside. Reports have emerged that some of those who arrived in western Aleppo were arrested by the Syrian regime, among them *Aleppo Today* journalist Ahmad Mustafa and White Helmets volunteer Abdulhadi Kamel; others were forcibly disappeared and some were forcibly conscripted into the Syrian army.[37]

HOMS, DARAYYA, AND EASTERN ALEPPO: A NON-EXHAUSTIVE LIST

The study presented above of Homs, Darayya, and Eastern Aleppo—once pro-opposition strongholds—sheds light on a nationwide policy of forced evacuations employed by the Syrian regime to consolidate control militarily and politically, to silence dissent and punish those partaking in it, and to change the sectarian and political demographics of Syria. Recognizing that the regime would no longer be able to assert control over civilians whose family members it has arrested, forcibly disappeared, displaced, and killed, it has instead opted to change the population it does control into one made of loyalists.

But Homs, Darayya, and Eastern Aleppo do not comprise the exhaustive list of localities[38] that would become the target of the Syrian regime's displacement campaigns. From Madaya in April 2017 to Eastern Ghouta in April 2018,[39] Syrian government forces and their allies subjected entire populations to medieval sieges under which civilians were forced to "surrender or starve" time and time again. These sieges were weaponized—in part as a result of the involvement of foreign actors like Russia, Iran, and Hezbollah—and designed to bring about "evacuation deals" that would lead to the displacement of pro-opposition fighters and civilians from their homes. At least some of these "evacuation deals" came about as a result of brokering by foreign powers, and a few of the "evacuations" were carried out under observation by UN officials.

Today, the regime continues to partake in steps that threaten to formalize the forced political and sectarian demographic changes initiated during the war including the creation of logistical, legal, and political obstacles that make it near impossible for many original residents to return to their homes.

THE PROHIBITION ON FORCED DISPLACEMENT IN
INTERNATIONAL LAW

Per the definition set forth in the UNHCR Handbook for the Protection of Internally Displaced Persons, "forced displacement occurs when individuals and communities have been forced or obliged to flee or to leave their homes or places of habitual residence as a result of or in order to avoid the effects of events or situations such as armed conflict, generalized violence, human rights abuses, natural or man-made disasters, and/or development projects. It both includes situations where people have fled as well as situations where people have been forcibly removed from their homes, evicted or relocated to another place not of their choosing, whether by State or non-State actors. The defining factor is the absence of will or consent."[40]

International humanitarian law prohibits forced displacement. Specifically, "parties to a non-international armed conflict may not order the displacement of the civilian population, in whole or in part, for reasons related to the conflict, unless the security of the civilians involved or imperative military reasons so demand."[41] For purposes of this definition, "ordering" does not only include directly ordering the population to leave their homes, but also includes ordering measures that would create circumstances that leave the population with no choice but to leave their homes; these measures "may include for example subjecting inhabited areas to bombardment or targeting infrastructure essential for the wellbeing of civilians such as water pumping stations, schools, medical units or food outlets."[42]

Because there are rare cases in which the temporary displacement of civilians in times of war may be necessary; the prohibition on forced displacement allows for two narrow exceptions when "the security of the civilians involved or imperative military reasons so demand." Although Syria is not a signatory, looking to Additional Protocol II to the Geneva Conventions and the International Committee of the Red Cross's (ICRC's) commentary helps explain the scope of the exceptions. The ICRC commentary reads: "The exception of 'imperative military reasons' can never cover cases of removal of the civilian population in order to persecute it."[43] A document by the United Nations Human Rights Office of the High Commissioner adds: "it cannot be justified by political motives such as seeking to gain more effective control over a dissident group."[44]

In the rare situation in which one of these two narrow exceptions is met, "any displacement must be temporary and as brief as possible with civilians allowed to return voluntarily in safety and in dignity to their homes as soon as the danger warranting their displacement ceases."[45] In any case, international humanitarian law conceives of displacement as a policy of last resort; the Guiding Principles on Internal Displacement read: "Prior to any decision requiring the displacement of persons, the authorities concerned shall ensure that all feasible alternatives are explored in order to avoid displacement altogether. Where no alternatives exist, all measures shall be taken to minimize displacement and its adverse effects."[46]

In the world of international criminal law, although there is currently no international criminal tribunal that has jurisdiction over the abuses being perpetrated in Syria, it remains instructive to look at the statutes of the International Criminal Court (ICC) and other courts to identify the magnitude of the crime at hand. "Ordering the displacement of the civilian population for reasons related to the conflict, unless the security of the civilians involved or imperative military reasons so demand," constitutes a war crime in non-international armed conflicts per the Rome State of the ICC. If committed as part of a widespread or systematic attack directed against the civilian population,[47] "deportation" can also constitute a crime against humanity, as per the Rome Statute and the statutes of the International Criminal Tribunal for the Former Yugoslavia, the International Criminal Tribunal for Rwanda, and the Special Court for Sierra Leone.[48]

Also vital to note is that while this chapter focuses specifically on the forced displacement that came about as a result of "surrender or starve" campaigns and "evacuation deals," the crime of forced displacement, both in Syria and across the world, has been and continues to be committed in conjunction with a range of other crimes not discussed here, which are similarly prohibited under international law and can similarly be prosecuted in international courts. They include, but are not limited to, the intentional directing of attacks against the civilian population, the use of starvation as a method of warfare, the intentional directing of attacks on humanitarian assistance personnel and vehicles, and pillaging.[49] Thus, in cases in which forced displacement is not prosecuted as a crime in and of itself, it can still be prosecuted via other crimes.

Additionally important to add is that while those who were forced to leave their homes as part of these "evacuation deals" have undergone the crime of forced displacement, it is also true that those who are forced to leave their homes throughout any point of the "surrender or starve" campaigns—a policy put in place to bring about these very "evacuation deals"—have also undergone this crime.

Finally, forced displacement implicates violations of international human rights law, set forth in treaties that Syria has acceded to including the International Covenant on Civil and Political Rights[50] and the International Covenant on Economic, Social, and Cultural Rights,[51] as well as explained in the Guiding Principles on Internal Displacement.[52] These rights and principles include, but are not limited to, the right to life, dignity, liberty, and security; the right to freedom of movement; the freedom to choose one's residence; and the right not to be arbitrarily deprived of property and possessions.

"EVACUATION DEALS" IN SYRIA:
A FORM OF FORCED DISPLACEMENT

At the beginning of March 2017, the Independent International Commission of Inquiry on the Syrian Arab Republic released a report on the fall of eastern Aleppo. Among other findings, the report concluded:

> After the recapture of eastern Aleppo, the Government and armed groups reached an agreement that led to the evacuation of the remaining population. Under the terms of the agreement, which follows previous similar agreements, including those applied to Darayya and Moadamiyah in August 2016, civilians had no option to remain. Many were permitted to move to western Aleppo, while others were transported to Idlib, where they live without adequate living conditions and in fear of future attacks. Such agreements amount to the war crime of forced displacement of the civilian population.[53]

The report's finding is significant in that it determines that the "evacuation deal" signed in eastern Aleppo constitutes the crime of forced displacement—a crime that occurs in contravention of international humanitarian law, international criminal law, and international human rights law. The report's language additionally seems to imply that "evacuation deals" occurring under similar contexts, be they prior to the time of the fall of eastern Aleppo or ones more recent, also occurred and continue to occur in violation of international law. In fact, in a later report published in May 2018, the commission more explicitly confirms: "...there are reasonable grounds to believe that parties to the conflict committed the war crime of forced displacement of civilians from eastern Aleppo city in December 2016, Madaya (Rif Damascus) in April 2017, Barza, Tishreen, and Qabun (eastern Damascus) in May 2017, and Fu'ah and Kafraya villages (Idlib) in May 2017."[54] The commission's findings echo what human rights[55] defenders[56] and legal observers[57] have been concluding in the time since the very first "evacuation deal" was signed—that it is improper and inaccurate to call what the Syrian regime refers to as "evacuation deals" without an understanding of the relationship between these deals and the crime of forced displacement.

From an international humanitarian law perspective, Syrian government forces and allies took actions, including but not limited to the besieging of areas, the targeting of civilians and civilian centers, and the use of starvation as a method of warfare, in furtherance of an intent to forcibly displace the population. This displacement did not occur for the sake of either of the two narrowly-defined exceptions: the "security of the civilians involved" or "imperative military reasons." Rather, the displacement occurred as a result of consistent violations to the security of the civilian populations and subjected these same populations to violations of security by transferring them either to government-controlled areas where they could be persecuted for their politi-

86 *Mai El-Sadany*

cal opinions or to opposition-controlled areas that could be bombarded by barrel bombs and airstrikes. Additionally, the displacement occurred in furtherance of a policy of sectarian and political demographic change—not "imperative military reason," but rather, in pursuit of "political motives like gaining control over a dissident group."

From an international criminal law perspective, a compelling case can be made that these "evacuation deals" constitute the war crime of forced displacement. If a court of law were additionally able to establish that this forced displacement occurred as part of a widespread or systematic attack directed against the civilian population—a finding that is likely possible in light of the Syrian regime's continued reliance on these forced "evacuation deals" as a means by which to change the political and sectarian demographics of the country and consolidate power—the crime against humanity of "deportation" could additionally be prosecuted. This is in addition, of course, to the other war crimes and crimes against humanity that the Syrian regime and its allies perpetrated alongside, in pursuit of, and as a result of forced displacement.

Finally, from an international human rights law perspective, there is no doubt that the Syrian regime continues to violate its treaty obligations when it forces its civilian populations to leave their homes as a result of sustained sieges that last for months; it does so in violation of numerous internationally-recognized, fundamental rights and freedoms.

CONCLUSION

Today, the Syrian regime is beginning to shop around for reconstruction assistance to rebuild the country; it is passing and implementing housing, land, and property (HLP) laws that allow it to repossess the property of displaced persons, as well as what it deems to be "rubble"[58]; and it is refusing for reentry and arresting, forcibly conscripting, and in some cases, torturing and killing individuals perceived to be in opposition to the government.[59] Collectively, these economic, legal, and policy measures help formalize and institutionalize the impact of the forced displacement and demographic change that took place during the war in part as a result of the regime's "surrender or starve" campaigns and "evacuation deals."

As countries, businesses, international entities, and organizations consider any form of engagement with the Syrian state, they would do well to first understand the ways in which this displacement has manifested—both in order to avoid furthering the impact of or becoming implicated in the crime of forced displacement, as well as to begin to propose, advocate for, and implement policy-oriented and legal recommendations that tackle the needs of even a subset of those affected by this crime.[60]

While reports and documentation efforts, including those put forth by independent monitoring initiatives like Siege Watch[61] and UN-affiliated bodies like the Independent International Commission of Inquiry on the Syrian Arab Republic,[62] are beginning to piece together a narrative of the ways in which forced displacement took place across Syria, documenting and assessing the needs of displaced persons—as victims of the crime of forced displacement—remains a key first step. Questions like, how and where forced displacement took place; who the victims and perpetrators of forced displacement were; the extent of violations that forcibly displaced persons underwent before, during, and after the displacement took place; and how these violations manifest in and implicate issue areas like HLP today, remain insufficiently addressed.

Tackling these questions and speaking to victims will help bring about victim-centric solutions, contributing to an internationally-recognized and well-substantiated narrative of what happened, who was involved, and how this remains relevant today; creating a space for displaced persons to tell their stories and be heard; providing civil society and humanitarian organizations with the data necessary to inform their work to remedy and reverse the impact of forced displacement on the population; and empowering advocates and legal practitioners to propose and work toward justice-oriented solutions and accountability, both inside the courtroom and outside of it.

But it will also underscore areas that are in need of a longer-term and more systematic response, be it in the form of amendments to domestic legislation that threaten to dispossess displaced Syrians of their property, recommendations for property restitution and civil documentation policies that must be put in place when a domestic space allows for it, the creation of HLP and human rights due diligence practices for businesses looking to invest in a postwar Syria, and institutional reform in the role that entities like the United Nations play in future siege and forced displacement crises.

NOTES

1. Saad Hajo, "The Green Bus," *The Creative Memory,* April 19, 2017, http://www.creativememory.org/?p=160302.
2. "Chinese Buses Witness the Ins and Outs of the Syrian War," *Enab Baladi,* December 17, 2016, http://english.enabbaladi.net/archives/2016/12/chinese-buses-witness-ins-outs-syrian-war/.
3. James Denselow, "Syria's Green Buses: Symbol of a Seismic Shift," *Al-Jazeera,* March 22, 2017, http://www.aljazeera.com/indepth/opinion/2017/03/syria-green-buses-symbol-seismic-shift-170321120600909.html.
4. Anne Barnard and Hwaida Saad, "Stark Choice for Syrians in Rebel Areas: 'Doom' or the Green Bus," *New York Times,* October 29, 2016, https://www.nytimes.com/2016/10/30/world/middleeast/once-propelled-by-hope-for-a-modern-syria-green-buses-now-run-on-tears.html?_r=0&module=ArrowsNav&contentCollection=Middle%20East&action=keypress&region=FixedLeft&pgtype=article.

5. Nicholas Blanford, "Surrender or Starve: Rebel-Held Syrian Towns Face Brutal Choice," *UPI,* January 9, 2017, http://www.upi.com/Top_News/Opinion/2017/01/09/Surrender-or-starve-Rebel-held-Syrian-towns-face-brutal-choice/1011483975945/.

6. Emma Beals, "Syria's Cruel 'Reconciliations,'" *The Daily Beast,* April 21, 2017, http://www.thedailybeast.com/syrias-cruel-reconciliations.

7. Anne Barnard and Hwaida Saad, "Stark Choice for Syrians in Rebel Areas: 'Doom' or the Green Bus," *New York Times,* October 29, 2016, https://www.nytimes.com/2016/10/30/world/middleeast/once-propelled-by-hope-for-a-modern-syria-green-buses-now-run-on-tears.html?_r=0&module=ArrowsNav&contentCollection=Middle%20East&action=keypress&region=FixedLeft&pgtype=article.

8. James Denselow, "Syria's Green Buses: Symbol of a Seismic Shift," *Al-Jazeera,* March 22, 2017, http://www.aljazeera.com/indepth/opinion/2017/03/syria-green-buses-symbol-seismic-shift-170321120600909.html.

9. Independent International Commission of Inquiry on the Syrian Arab Republic, "Sieges as a Weapon of War," *OHCHR,* May 29, 2018, https://www.ohchr.org/Documents/HRBodies/HRCouncil/CoISyria/PolicyPaperSieges_29May2018.pdf.

10. Independent International Commission of Inquiry on the Syrian Arab Republic, "Sieges as a Weapon of War," *OHCHR,* May 29, 2018, https://www.ohchr.org/Documents/HRBodies/HRCouncil/CoISyria/PolicyPaperSieges_29May2018.pdf.

11. "No Going Back: Forced Displacement in the Syrian Conflict," *The Syrian American Council,* February 8, 2017, http://www.sacouncil.com/no_going_back_forced.

12. "No Return to Homs," *The Syria Institute,* February 21, 2017, http://syriainstitute.org/wp-content/uploads/2017/02/PAX_REPORT_Homs_FINAL_web_single_page.pdf.

13. "No Going Back: Forced Displacement in the Syrian Conflict," *The Syrian American Council,* February 8, 2017, http://www.sacouncil.com/no_going_back_forced.

14. "No Return to Homs," *The Syria Institute,* February 21, 2017, http://syriainstitute.org/wp-content/uploads/2017/02/PAX_REPORT_Homs_FINAL_web_single_page.pdf.

15. "Regime Endorses Seizure of Property in Homs by Shiites and Alawites," *Syrian Observer,* April 10, 2015, http://syrianobserver.com/EN/News/28994/Regime_Endorses_Seizure_Property_Homs_Shiites_Alawites.

16. Martin Chulov, "Iran Repopulates Syria with Shia Muslims to Help Tighten Regime's Control," *The Guardian,* January 13, 2017, https://www.theguardian.com/world/2017/jan/13/irans-syria-project-pushing-population-shifts-to-increase-influence.

17. "No Return to Homs," *The Syria Institute,* February 21, 2017, http://syriainstitute.org/wp-content/uploads/2017/02/PAX_REPORT_Homs_FINAL_web_single_page.pdf.

18. "Out of Sight, Out of Mind: The Aftermath of Syria's Sieges," *Siege Watch,* March 2019, https://siegewatch.org/wp-content/uploads/2015/10/pax-siege-watch-final-report-spread.pdf.

19. "Crimes against Humanity and War Crimes Are the Reason Behind the Forced Migration in Darayya," *Syrian Network for Human Rights,* August 31, 2016, http://sn4hr.org/wp-content/pdf/english/Crimes_against_humanity_forced_displacement_for_Daraya_en.pdf.

20. United Nations' Under-Secretary-General for Humanitarian Affairs and Emergency Relief Coordinator, Stephen O'Brien, referred to the city as "Syria's capital of barrel bombs."

21. "Syria: 'We Leave or We Die': Forced Displacement Under Syria's 'Reconciliation' Agreements," *Amnesty International,* November 13, 2017, https://www.amnesty.org/en/documents/mde24/7309/2017/en/.

22. Anne Barnard, "Residents Abandon Daraya as Government Seizes a Symbol of Syria's Rebellion," *New York Times,* August 26, 2016, https://www.nytimes.com/2016/08/27/world/middleeast/syria-daraya-falls-symbol-rebellion.html.

23. "Syria: 'We Leave or We Die': Forced Displacement Under Syria's 'Reconciliation' Agreements," *Amnesty International,* November 13, 2017, https://www.amnesty.org/en/documents/mde24/7309/2017/en/.

24. "Syria: 'We Leave or We Die': Forced Displacement Under Syria's 'Reconciliation' Agreements," *Amnesty International,* November 13, 2017, https://www.amnesty.org/en/documents/mde24/7309/2017/en/.

25. "Displacement and Demographic Change Create New Realities in Syria," *The Syrian Observer*, March 17, 2017, http://www.syrianobserver.com/EN/Features/32483/Displacement_Demographic_Change_Create_New_Realities_Syria.

26. Haid Haid, "Where Is Home for the Permanently Displaced Citizens of Darayya," *Heinrich Boll Stiftung*, September 2018, https://lb.boell.org/sites/default/files/daraya_paper_-_haid_haid.pdf.

27. Leila Al Shami, "Exile: Forced Displacement and Demographic Change in Syria," *Leila's Blog*, March 25, 2017, https://leilashami.wordpress.com/2017/03/25/exile-forced-displacement-and-demographic-change-in-syria/.

28. "Evacuation of Syria's Aleppo Was a War Crime, Says UN Panel," *AP*, March 1, 2017, http://www.belfasttelegraph.co.uk/news/world-news/evacuation-of-syrias-aleppo-was-a-war-crime-says-un-panel-35493648.html.

29. "Eyes on Aleppo: Visual Evidence Analysis of Human Rights Violations Committed in Aleppo [July – Dec 2016]," *Bellingcat*, March 29, 2017, https://www.bellingcat.com/news/mena/2017/03/29/eyes-aleppo-visual-evidence-analysis-human-rights-violations-committed-aleppo-july-dec-2016/.

30. Chris Hughes, "No Mercy for Children as Assad Vows to Keep Bombing until Aleppo Is 'Cleansed of Terrorists'," *The Mirror*, October 14, 2016, http://www.mirror.co.uk/news/world-news/no-mercy-children-assad-vows-9046927.

31. "No Going Back: Forced Displacement in the Syrian Conflict," *The Syrian American Council*, February 8, 2017, http://www.sacouncil.com/no_going_back_forced.

32. Kareem Shaheen, "Iran-Backed Militias Block Aleppo Evacuation as Shelling Resumes," *The Guardian*, December 14, 2016, https://www.theguardian.com/world/2016/dec/14/aleppo-residents-evacuation-uncertainty-ceasefire-deal-assad.

33. "Special Report on the Evacuation of Civilians from East Aleppo," *Violations Documentation Center*, January 6, 2017, http://vdc-sy.net/Website/wp-content/uploads/2017/01/Aleppo-report-En-.pdf.

34. Nabih Bulos, "The Evacuation Buses Finally Arrived—But Aleppo Has Descended Back into Violence," *Los Angeles Times*, December 14, 2016, http://www.latimes.com/world/la-fg-aleppo-battle-20161214-story.html.

35. Lisa Barrington and Suleiman Al-Khalidi, "Gunmen Burn Buses, Aleppo Convoy Goes Through," *Reuters*, December 18, 2016, http://www.reuters.com/article/us-mideast-crisis-syria-idUSKBN1451JG.

36. "Breaking Aleppo," *The Atlantic Council*, February 2017, http://www.publications.atlanticcouncil.org/breakingaleppo/wp-content/uploads/2017/02/BreakingAleppo.pdf.

37. Leila Al Shami, "Exile: Forced Displacement and Demographic Change in Syria," *Leila's Blog*, March 25, 2017, https://leilashami.wordpress.com/2017/03/25/exile-forced-displacement-and-demographic-change-in-syria/.

38. "Syria's Divisions Crystallize with Latest Evacuations," *Bloomberg*, April 14, 2017, https://www.bloomberg.com/news/articles/2017-04-14/urgent-syrian-deal-to-evacuate-tens-of-thousands-of-people-begins.

39. "Out of Sight, Out of Mind: The Aftermath of Syria's Sieges," *Siege Watch*, March 2019, https://siegewatch.org/wp-content/uploads/2015/10/pax-siege-watch-final-report-spread.pdf.

40. "Handbook for the Protection of Internally Displaced Persons," *UNHCR*, http://www.unhcr.org/4794b2d52.pdf.

41. ICRC, Customary International Humanitarian Law: Volume 1: Rules, Rule 129, https://ihl-databases.icrc.org/customary-ihl/eng/docs/v1_rul_rule129#Fn_11_28.

42. "Transfer of the Civilian Population in International Law," *United Nations Human Rights Office of the High Commissioner*, January 2017, https://www.humanitarianresponse.info/system/files/documents/files/population_transfer_legal_note_-_final_-_en.pdf.

43. ICRC, Customary International Humanitarian Law: Volume 1: Rules, Rule 129, https://ihl-databases.icrc.org/customary-ihl/eng/docs/v1_rul_rule129#Fn_11_28.

44. "Transfer of the Civilian Population in International Law," *United Nations Human Rights Office of the High Commissioner*, January 2017, https://www.humanitarianresponse.info/system/files/documents/files/population_transfer_legal_note_-_final_-_en.pdf.

45. "Transfer of the Civilian Population in International Law," *United Nations Human Rights Office of the High Commissioner,* January 2017, https://www.humanitarianresponse. info/system/files/documents/files/population_transfer_legal_note_-_final_-_en.pdf.

46. "The Guiding Principles on Internal Displacement," *United Nations,* September 2004, http://www.unhcr.org/en-us/protection/idps/43ce1cff2/guiding-principles-internal-displacement.html.

47. Federico Andreu-Guzmán, "Criminal Justice and Forced Displacement: International and National Perspectives," *ICTJ,* June 2013, https://www.ictj.org/sites/default/files/ICTJ-Research-Brief-Displacement-Criminal-Justice-Andreu-Guzman.pdf.

48. "Transfer of the Civilian Population in International Law," *United Nations Human Rights Office of the High Commissioner,* January 2017, https://www.humanitarianresponse. info/system/files/documents/files/population_transfer_legal_note_-_final_-_en.pdf.

49. Federico Andreu-Guzmán, "Criminal Justice and Forced Displacement: International and National Perspectives," *ICTJ,* June 2013, https://www.ictj.org/sites/default/files/ICTJ-Research-Brief-Displacement-Criminal-Justice-Andreu-Guzman.pdf.

50. Syria acceded to the International Covenant on Civil and Political Rights on April 21, 1969.

51. Syria acceded to the International Covenant on Economic, Social, and Cultural Rights on April 21, 1969.

52. "The Guiding Principles on Internal Displacement," *United Nations,* September 2004, http://www.unhcr.org/en-us/protection/idps/43ce1cff2/guiding-principles-internal-displacement.html.

53. "Report of the Independent International Commission of Inquiry on the Syrian Arab Republic 'Special Inquiry into the Events in Aleppo,'" A/HRC/34/64, *United Nations Human Rights, Office of the High Commissioner,* March 1, 2017, http://www.ohchr.org/EN/HRBodies/HRC/IICISyria/Pages/IndependentInternationalCommission.aspx.

54. Independent International Commission of Inquiry on the Syrian Arab Republic, "Sieges as a Weapon of War," *OHCHR,* May 29, 2018, https://www.ohchr.org/Documents/HRBodies/HRCouncil/CoISyria/PolicyPaperSieges_29May2018.pdf.

55. "PHR Calls Forced Evacuation of Syrian Suburb a War Crime," *Physicians for Human Rights,* September 2, 2016, http://physiciansforhumanrights.org/press/press-releases/phr-calls-forced-evacuation-of-syrian-suburb-a-war-crime.html?print=t?referrer=https://www.google.com/.

56. Ben Taub, "Aleppo's Evacuation Is a Crime against Humanity," *The New Yorker,* December 22, 2016, http://www.newyorker.com/news/daily-comment/aleppos-evacuation-is-a-crime-against-humanity.

57. "Forced Displacement in Syria and International Accountability," *Syria Justice and Accountability Centre,* March 23, 2017, https://syriaaccountability.org/updates/2017/03/23/forced-displacement-in-syria-and-international-accountability/.

58. Sage Smiley, Noura Hourani, and Reem Ahmad,"'A new Syria': Law 10 Reconstruction Projects to Commence in Damascus, Backed by Arsenal of Demolition, Expropriation Legislation," *Syria Direct,* November 19, 2018, https://syriadirect.org/news/%E2%80%98a-new-syria%E2%80%99-law-10-reconstruction-projects-to-commence-in-damascus-backed-by-arsenal-of-demolition-expropriation-legislation/.

59. Louisa Loveluck, "Assad Urged Syrians to Come Home. Many Are Being Welcomed with Arrest and Interrogation." *Washington Post,* June 2, 2019, http://www.washingtonpost.com/world/assad-urged-syrian-refugees-to-come-home-many-are-being-welcomed-with-arrest-and-interrogation/2019/06/02/54bd696a-7bea-11e9-b1f3-b233fe5811ef_story.html.

60. "Statement of Eminent Jurists on Legal Obligations When Supporting Reconstruction in Syria," September 24, 2018, https://www.business-humanrights.org/sites/default/files/documents/Eminents%20Jurists%20Statement_Syria%20reconstruction.pdf.

61. "Siege Watch," *The Syria Institute,* https://siegewatch.org/.

62. "Independent International Commission of Inquiry on the Syrian Arab Republic," *OHCHR,* https://www.ohchr.org/en/hrbodies/hrc/iicisyria/pages/independentinternational commission.aspx.

Chapter Six

The False Allure of Syrian "Local Ceasefires"

Mohammed Alaa Ghanem

American policymakers and diplomatic officials worldwide often show a highly flawed understanding of the local deals "agreed" upon by the Assad regime and Syrian opposition groups. These deals, typically called "local ceasefires" or "evacuations," often earn praise simply because they (temporarily) reduce violence or suffering in a given location. UN humanitarian operations coordinator John Ging, for instance, praised the so-called "evacuation agreement" that evicted residents from the City of Homs in mid-2014 as "evidence of what can be done."[1]

Policy analysts have also incorrectly floated local ceasefires as a potential way forward. In 2014, former Obama Administration officials Steven Simon and Jonathan Stevenson posited the Homs ceasefire as an exemplar of "the classic 'inkblot' strategy" in which "such ceasefires could turn into more lasting arrangements for local governance."[2] Yezid Sayigh similarly argued that a national ceasefire would "embolden and empower civilian communities . . . making it harder for their leaders and commanders to order a return to armed conflict."[3]

More recently, a Russian-proposed plan for "de-escalation zones" has gained currency in Washington, D.C. While framed as a nationwide initiative, this plan as well is essentially a collection of local ceasefires in the four main opposition pockets—Idlib Province and its environs, Daraa and Quneitra Provinces, the East Ghouta suburbs of Damascus, and the northern suburbs of Homs City. Trump Administration officials have framed the ceasefires as a way to reduce levels of violence while putting aside broader questions of Assad's legitimacy.

However, these analyses fundamentally misunderstand the origins and purposes of local ceasefires. Such ceasefires serve two core purposes for the Assad regime. First, they enable the regime to regain control of areas—especially densely populated urban areas—that it is unable to conquer militarily, by besieging and starving the populations in these areas until local rebels agree to forced population transfers. This has occurred in the Province of Homs and in many suburbs of Damascus.

Second, local ceasefires relieve the Assad regime's severe manpower shortage. Due to its status as a minority regime[4] that advances the interests of (and exploits) the minority Alawite sect, Assad regime forces have been severely outnumbered for the duration of the Syrian conflict. This means that the regime "must pick its battles, fighting aggressively in some places and just holding on in others."[5] Even in areas that do not see sectarian cleansing initially, local ceasefires help to achieve that goal. In recent months, a number of areas that were party to local ceasefire agreements were attacked anew, especially the East Ghouta "de-escalation zone" that is now under intensified siege and escalating bombardment.[6]

CITY OF HOMS: THE CEASEFIRE THAT LEFT A "GHOST TOWN"

The City of Homs was the first major case of sectarian cleansing following a long-term siege and "local ceasefire." The city emerged as a center of the pro-democracy protests in 2011, earning the moniker "Capital of the Revolution," and most areas were beyond regime control by early 2012. But the regime gradually tightened a siege from 2012–2013 and, by mid-2014, residents had gone years without humanitarian access. Many civilians were reduced to eating weeds and leaves to survive. Regime forces launched a massive offensive on the city in April 2014, and rebels agreed to a "ceasefire" and "evacuation" from Homs the following month under threat of total extermination.

In part due to laudatory UN statements regarding the outcome in Homs, so-called "local ceasefires" first reached the attention of Western policymakers as a potential "solution" to the conflict around this time. But the Homs ceasefire was fraught with problems from the beginning. One anecdote I heard from the ground at the time is indicative.

Within a week after the Homs deal, a displaced former resident returned to her home neighborhood, which was once a center of opposition activity, and was pleasantly surprised to find her house intact. She took a short trip to her temporary residence to prepare to move back home, and then returned to her house in Homs City—but the house had been thoroughly looted. When she tried to move back into her old home anyway, pro-regime paramilitaries with Assad's "National Defense Forces" showed up at her door and demanded that she leave. She returned to a refugee camp once again, her prospects of returning more distant than ever before.

The circumstances of this case point strongly to the conclusion that pro-regime paramilitaries looted and took over this former Homs resident's home, and indeed, many other incidents of looting were caught on camera. The last rebel fighters to leave Homs managed to film regime soldiers looting valuable cooking gas canisters from private residences. Other video footage showed regime forces, in full military fatigues, gathering the looted canisters in a central area.

The looting in Homs had strong sectarian undertones. Following the forced displacement of Homs residents in both the "ceasefires" and in earlier regime military victories, stolen items from Homs residences reappeared at "Sunni markets" in pro-regime areas at bargain prices. These "Sunni markets" are so called by locals because regime supporters often come from Assad's Alawite sect and tend to regard the Syrian uprising as a revolt by the country's Sunni majority. At the markets, Western journalists have observed buyers and sellers alike refer to the merchandise as "spoils of war."[7]

Furthermore, while the eviction of one Homs resident is merely an anec-dote, evidence points to a far more systematic effort at forced displacement. On July 5, 2013, a suspicious fire broke out at the Land Registry building of Homs. Only the top floors, which housed the land registry archives for all Homs residents, were affected. Regime troops were stationed on the lower floors, but did not respond to the fire. With the destruction of the land archives, all records of residency for displaced Homs residents were wiped out. This left former Homs residents dependent on regime good graces for their right to return home.

In most cases, such good graces were not forthcoming. A report by The Syria Institute, which included interviews with displaced former Homs resi-dents, quotes one interviewee as saying that Homsis need regime permission to return home and that most displaced residents "do not dare to ask."[8] In the years since the sectarian cleansing, numerous media reports have described the former opposition areas of Homs as a "ghost town."[9]

The Assad regime has made active and parallel efforts to facilitate a stronger presence for its Alawite and Shiite sectarian affiliates in former opposition areas of Homs. Opposition sources indicate that Iran has pur-chased large tracts of land in the southern suburbs of Homs, where rebel fighters had a strong presence until Hezbollah—Iran's Lebanese Shiite proxy—dislodged them in mid-2013. Local leaders in multiple former oppo-sition neighborhoods of Homs itself have also reported the resettlement of Alawite families in their areas.

DAMASCUS SUBURBS: STARVE, SURRENDER, AND FLEE

The Damascus suburbs are a second area that saw widespread starvation sieges, followed by "local ceasefires" and then sectarian cleansing. In Damascus's suburbs, the regime's manpower-related motive for local ceasefires was particularly important due to the presence of wide swathes of anti-Assad population centers within striking distance of the capital. These densely-populated areas often proved highly resistant to regime conquest. To help relieve its manpower shortage, the regime was particularly keen on neutralizing potential launch points for a rebel assault on the capital Damascus.[10]

Rebels, particularly in the southern suburbs of Damascus, had launched a massive assault on the capital Damascus in the summer of 2012 and thrown the regime into disarray. Although the regime was able to recover and stop the assault, it suffered massive losses in northern and eastern Syria while making frantic redeployments toward the capital. The regime's ability to besiege, and then coerce local populations near Damascus into ceasefires with the brutal choice of "kneel or starve," allowed the regime to later regain the initiative in northern Syria, especially in and around Aleppo City.

Particularly grueling sieges took place in the southern suburbs and neighborhoods of Damascus due in part to their high strategic importance. Sieges on southern Damascus suburbs and neighborhoods such as Moadamiya, Darayya, Yarmouk, and Babbila began in late 2012 and were gradually tightened throughout 2013. The first "local ceasefire" to be signed in this area, and perhaps in all of Syria, was in Moadamiya town in October 2013 after locals had been—as in Homs—reduced to eating grass and leaves to survive.[11] The Yarmouk Palestinian Refugee Camp and nearby Babbila followed suit in early 2014, with tens of thousands flocking to receive the first aid shipment to Yarmouk in a scene that drew global attention to the camp's plight. Darayya never signed a ceasefire and was subjected to extremely intensive bombardments, earning the grim moniker "The Capital of Barrel Bombs."

These ceasefires, at least initially, did not lead to forced displacement. But because these deals were so unequal, they were subject to a ratcheting effect. Local councils and fighters in various locales of Damascus's suburbs had only "agreed" to local ceasefires because the regime had already blocked their food access. While ceasefires were supposed to restore food access, they in no way impeded the regime's ability to restrict it anew. At any time, the regime had the ability to reinstate the siege and extract further concessions from starving populations. Local ceasefires therefore had the effect of helping to cement the starvation sieges that had brought them about and further weaken the rebels.

For instance, in Moadamiya, regime forces initially offered food to townspeople if rebels ceased attacks and flew the Assad flag. But the demands escalated over time so that by the end of the process, rebels had been coerced into leaving urban centers and relinquishing their heavy weapons. In Yarmouk, civilians were again dying of starvation only weeks after a ceasefire was signed, because the regime simply reneged on its promise of restoring aid access. And in the nearby Babbila area, the regime drastically curtailed aid access after residents refused regime demands—which were not present in the original ceasefire deal—to grant regime troops free usage of a local police station as a base.

Despite the ceasefires signed in both Yarmouk and Babbila, the two areas are under siege today, with conditions worsened because ISIS set up a base in the adjoining Hajar al-Aswad neighborhood and used that base to attack Yarmouk. An "evacuation" agreement saw hundreds of residents[12] leave Yarmouk to escape regime siege in early 2014, and a second such agreement saw further evacuations in 2016.[13] Yarmouk, which housed 150,000 residents before the war, now houses under 10,000 people. Meanwhile, the humanitarian situation in Babbila and its environs had so deteriorated that town representatives approached the regime for a new "ceasefire" in early 2015.[14]

The regime also reneged on the "ceasefire" in Moadamiya—after forcing tens of thousands of IDPs to return to the town and driving up the population from around 6,000 to over 45,000, in a move widely viewed by activists as a means to overwhelm the town's local council. In April 2015, despite the ceasefire that was supposed to be in effect in Moadamiya, regime negotiator Hassan Gandour issued a chilling ultimatum to Moadamiya residents:

All residents, whether civilians, political opposition (sic) or "Free Army" armed opposition must be evacuated unless the town returns to the bosom of the state in all senses of the term. If there is no mechanism to return the town to the bosom of the state . . . within at most fifteen days from the transmission of this message, then any individual found inside the town takes his life into his hands.

I recognize and speak now to the half-men, the semi-humans, who broker in blood and in crises, that you have triumphed and achieved your goal. But I warn you that one battle will not win the war; yes, it is a war, a war you wanted, and I swear to the Almighty God by the anguished cries of our women, children and fellow residents that we will take revenge and make you regret what you have done to our nation.[15]

The regime reinstated a full siege on Moadamiya in August 2015 and, buoyed by the Russian intervention in Syria the following month, resumed attacks on Moadamiya at the end of that year. Renewed attacks on Moadamiya enabled Russian and regime forces to cut the road between Moadamiya and neighboring Darayya in January 2016, which had the effect of tightening the siege on Darayya. Three months later, and under heavy diplomatic pressure, the regime only briefly allowed humanitarian aid in to the starving civilians of Darayya before launching a blistering military offensive—with over 200 barrel bombs dropped in the first five days—that led to the sectarian cleansing of the town in August 2016.[16]

As in Homs City in 2014, rebels in Darayya in 2016 agreed to a "cease-fire" and "evacuation" only after the regime threatened them with extermination unless they did so. The regime demanded that Darayya residents relocate specifically to Idlib, where hardline elements are stronger, and where Free Syrian Army-dominated rebels from Darayya were eventually abducted by Al-Qaeda militants. Reports from Darayya after the sectarian cleansing indicated that family members of fighters from Harakat al-Nujaba, an Iran-backed Iraqi militia with strong Shiite extremist leanings, had supplanted local residents. About 300 Moadamiya residents with Darayya origins were also evacuated to Idlib in September 2016.

BARZEH, WAER, AND WADI BARADA: BROKEN CEASEFIRES

In the case of Moadamiya, an agreed-upon ceasefire enabled the regime to concentrate its firepower on a neighboring town, renege on the ceasefire, and eventually conquer the nearby town. But in other cases, towns and neighborhoods that signed ceasefires themselves were overrun, their populations forcibly displaced years after their initial ceasefire deals with Assad were agreed upon. Ironically, many policy analysts who supported the "local ceasefire" concept when it first came into vogue in 2014 cited these towns, which were to be displaced years later, as examples of successful local ceasefires.

For instance, a London School of Economics study in 2014 concluded that the ceasefire in the Barzeh neighborhood of Damascus was "closer to a win-win situation"[17]—an outcome that, as the authors neglected to mention, was due to rebels' ability to block a key highway and the resulting increase in opposition leverage. Yet even in this neighborhood, problems emerged from the beginning. At the time, I responded to the study by highlighting the dangers of the Barzeh ceasefire in an article entitled, "The U.N is Walking into a Trap in Syria—Here's How to Avoid It."[18]

> Last week, a spokesman from the Barzeh Local Council denounced the regime for violating ceasefire terms. According to the spokesman, the regime has not withdrawn troops from the area and conducts regular arrest raids against civilians. Fuel supplies are running out, U.N. aid is being redirected, and the regime troop presence is actually increasing. Such a scenario is quite far from a win-win situation.

It turned out that the regime was only using the ceasefire as a temporary and strategic military tool. In early 2017, some three years after the initial ceasefire was agreed upon, and with the regime feeling renewed confidence following its conquest of Aleppo, regime forces attacked and seized Barzeh along with the neighboring towns of Qabun and Tishrin and forced thousands to depart for Idlib[19] in a new round of "ceasefire" agreements. This outcome was especially dangerous because it placed key smuggling routes from Damascus to the "East Ghouta" suburbs outside of opposition hands, leading to a dramatic worsening of the siege on the "East Ghouta" de-escalation zone and threatening over 400,000 civilians with malnutrition.

A similarly tragic outcome prevailed in the Homs neighborhood of Waer, which was cited by Simon and Stevenson in 2014 as a "workable modus vivendi" and as an exemplar of their proposed "inkblot" strategy in which "ceasefires turn into more lasting arrangements for local governance." Yet the siege of Waer—which became the last opposition-held neighborhood in the City of Homs after the 2014 Homs ceasefire—was never fully lifted, and bombardments never fully ceased. In December 2015, some 700 people left Waer in an "evacuation" due to the pressure on civilians after three years of starvation and siege.[20] Over 10,000 people left Waer in a much larger March 2017 "evacuation" that followed weeks of intensive airstrikes[21] by regime and Russian forces. At present, Waer is under Assad regime control.

A third location in which the regime reneged on a local ceasefire, attacking and forcibly displacing the population, is Wadi Barada (Barada Valley). In Wadi Barada, the ceasefire was more informal in nature, but the basic agreement was clear to both sides: if the regime tried to attack the Wadi, locals would close the Fijeh Spring that provided drinking water to the capital Damascus. Engineers at Fijeh Spring became de facto mediators[22] in the informal ceasefire between the Assad regime and rebel forces in the Wadi. The engineers relayed messages between the regime and Free Syrian Army rebels as well as providing daily updates on the status of the spring.

But in Wadi Barada, as in Barzeh and Waer, the regime felt emboldened by its conquest of Aleppo to ignore its longstanding agreement with locals in the area and launch a fresh assault. Indeed, soon after the fall of Aleppo in December 2016, regime forces began threatening the residents of Wadi that they would soon meet the fate of Aleppines. The regime spread the false rumor that Wadi residents were about to poison the spring, and then commenced a fierce bombing campaign that appeared to include the spring and nearby aquifer[23] as a target. In January 2017, regime forces bombed the aquifer, causing massive and perhaps-irreparable damage[24] to the Damascus water supply and water resources. As regime and Hezbollah forces slowly advanced, locals were forced to surrender; some 2,000 Wadi residents were "evacuated" from their homes[25] on January 30, and the area returned to regime control.

THE ZABADANI CEASEFIRE AND THE HORRORS OF MADAYA

Local ceasefires have a surface appeal because they at least temporarily reduce human suffering among the local population. However, a ceasefire signed not far from Wadi Barada, in the mountain town of Zabadani in September 2015, did not even meet this basic standard. Regime and Hezbollah forces launched their final assault on Zabadani in July 2015, unleashing a barrage of barrel bombs that United Nations Envoy to Syria Staffan de Mistura blamed for "unprecedented levels of destruction[26] and many deaths among the civilian population." The Assad regime and Hezbollah gradually advanced in Zabadani throughout July, while issuing periodic warnings for rebels to "surrender or die."[27] After two more months of fighting, rebels were forced into a United Nations-sponsored ceasefire in September.

Under the terms of the ceasefire,[28] rebels and "their family members who wished to leave" were to evacuate Zabadani for Idlib, while "hostile measures such as . . . closing the roads to Madaya" were to be ceased. But rather than honor these terms, pro-regime forces—and particularly Hezbollah—took far more sinister steps.

After most rebel fighters had left Zabadani for Idlib, Hezbollah moved into the city center and forced thousands of Syrian civilians to leave Zabadani for neighboring Madaya town. Some forcibly displaced Zabadani residents were explicitly told that they were being sent to Madaya to die from starvation.[29] Just three months later, and under a stifling siege, residents were reduced to eating leaves, stray animals, bugs, and trash to survive. Horrifying images from Madaya of skeletally thin children starving to death and crying for food triggered global outrage.[30]

By the time heavy diplomatic pressure forced the regime and Hezbollah to allow in a UN aid convoy, dozens of civilians had already died from starvation. Furthermore, despite the aid convoy, the suffering of civilians continued in the city, and numerous children[31] were seriously wounded[32] after being shot by Hezbollah snipers while trying to escape. By late 2016, Save the Children was reporting a rise in child suicide attempts[33] in Madaya due to the siege. An evacuation deal was finally reached[34] for Madaya in March 2017, leading thousands to be "evacuated"[35] from Madaya and Zabadani the following month, while some residents of the Kafraya and Fua towns besieged by rebel hardliners were also moved out in an arrangement that was dubbed the "Four Towns Agreement."

UN CULPABILITY

While local ceasefires have seldom improved the plight of civilians in the long-term, rebels and local councils had little choice but to agree to them in the face of overwhelming suffering and popular pressure to relieve starvation sieges. However, the United Nations, which is not subject to such pressures and has many potential paths to take regarding local ceasefires, has been remiss. UN diplomats and aid officials have in fact tacitly encouraged Assad's "starve and surrender" tactics in a number of ways.

First, the UN has consistently failed to stand up to regime sieges. During the Geneva diplomatic talks on Syria in February 2016, the UN Security Council passed a resolution that mentioned then-besieged Darayya by name[36] and demanded aid access. In May 2016, Secretary of State John Kerry even set a June 1st deadline[37] for access, with the implication that humanitarian airdrops by the United States would be on the table unless the UN was granted humanitarian access.

The regime "met" the deadline by allowing in only enough aid to feed a quarter of Daraya's residents. UN officials simply watched as regime operatives removed high-protein items from the aid packages, which reduced the aid convoy's overall effectiveness. UN officials didn't have to simply sit by as the regime gutted their aid convoy. They could have threatened to withdraw the convoy entirely, which might have triggered the humanitarian airdrops threatened by Kerry if his deadline went unmet.

Yet UN aid officials in Damascus chose to interpret their mandate in the most narrow and pro-regime manner possible. They allowed the regime to obey calls for humanitarian access in letter, but not in spirit. Similar complaints were heard from activists[38] in neighboring Moadamiya in late 2013, when the regime siege on that town was at its worst:

> You know what? This regime takes the prize for trickery. I'm not sure if most people outside Syria understand how amazingly deceitful this regime is with its media spin. I mean who would have thought you could take a straightforward demand, "Food, now," and twist it by basically saying: "You will take only these scrapings of food, directly from our bloodstained hands that have been murdering you, and you will do it now, on our degrading terms." Then, they will boast in front of the world that they're giving us "food," and try to destroy the momentum we are gaining for serious international humanitarian aid.

The Assad regime was indeed able to curb international momentum in Darayya, Moadamiya, and elsewhere—and UN aid officials played a role in assisting the process. Their dilatory approach toward delivering aid to regime-besieged areas has helped the regime to enforce its sieges; their subsequently vigorous efforts to "evacuate" civilians, after "ceasefires" are signed, aboard the now-notorious "green buses"[39] serve as de facto logistical support for sectarian cleansing.

Second, the UN has allowed its ostensibly objective estimates of the number of civilians under siege to be manipulated by the Assad regime. This problem was initially brought to light when images of abject suffering by besieged Madaya residents reached global attention in early 2016. It emerged that, only months prior, the UN Secretary General had released a report on the implementation of UN resolutions in Syria that did not list Madaya as besieged.[40]

Although over 2,000 residents were ultimately evacuated[41] from Zabadani and Madaya, the UN report in question found only 500 besieged persons in the district of Zabadani, where the towns of Zabadani and Madaya are both located. Only after images from Madaya triggered a global furor did the UN Office for the Coordination of Humanitarian Affairs (OCHA) admit being denied access to Madaya since October 2015,[42] which was soon after Hezbollah sent civilians to Madaya to starve. Scandal broke when a scathing *Foreign Policy* report published in late January 2016 found that OCHA, "after consulting the Syrian government, altered dozens of passages and omitted pertinent information to paint the government of Bashar al-Assad in a more favorable light."[43]

Third, and as discussed above, UN diplomacy has at times had the effect of encouraging Assad regime sieges and sectarian cleansing of civilians, as when UN aid coordinator John Ging praised the forced eviction of the residents of the City of Homs as "evidence of what can be done." These impacts are particularly relevant to the city of Aleppo, which saw some 100,000 civilians besieged and forcibly displaced in 2016.

As early as 2014, the specter of a starvation siege threatened Syria's largest city of Aleppo. Pro-regime forces had been on the cusp of besieging the city for some time, and the prospect of an imminent siege on the city[44] was well-discussed in the media.[45] It seemed as though Aleppo would soon be subjected to the same kind of "local ceasefire" that had been signed in Homs, Darayya, and elsewhere. Yet instead of treating this as a problem, de Mistura actually made the potential for a local ceasefire in Aleppo[46] the centerpiece of his new "freeze zones" initiative.[47]

While de Mistura undoubtedly did not intend for civilians in Aleppo to starve, the congruence between his "freeze zones" initiative and the regime's "local ceasefires" strategy left de Mistura's diplomacy highly vulnerable to regime exploitation—a fact that I warned his office of at the time.[48] Sure enough, Assad tried to fold the "freeze zones" initiative into his "local ceasefires" military strategy by accepting de Mistura's proposal and cutting the last supply line to Aleppo on the same day.[49] De Mistura chose to minimize developments on the ground and market this development as a diplomatic breakthrough; rebels launched a fierce counterattack and rejected the deal.[50]

The next time the fate of Aleppo hung in the balance was in summer 2016. After a year of additional efforts and heavy Russian support, pro-regime forces had managed to cut the last main rebel supply line[51] to Aleppo, which ran north of the city, in February 2016. But from July-August, rebels launched what they called the "Great Battle of Aleppo" and managed to open a new supply line from the south. Amid a regime counterattack and heavy fighting, de Mistura again called for a truce[52] in order to allow for aid deliveries to both regime and opposition areas of Aleppo.

But a problem with the proposal soon emerged: the UN insisted on delivering aid only through the Castello Road—the final road captured by the regime to besiege Aleppo—because it was "the safest and most direct route."[53] The UN ignored the objections of Aleppo activists and the democratically elected Aleppo City Council that by using the Castello Road, rather than the newly-opened southern road, the UN would be cementing the Assad regime's siege of Aleppo.[54]

Had the UN heeded these objections and insisted on the use of the southern Ramousa Road, or at least of both roads, to deliver aid, the regime's "starve and surrender" plan for Aleppo might have been thwarted. Instead, and as in the previous year, UN proposals for an Aleppo "freeze" or "truce" increased pressure on the opposition and meshed with the regime's forced displacement strategy. The regime soon recaptured the Ramousa Road, enforced a full siege, and launched a bloody final offensive that saw women kill themselves to avoid rape[55] by regime forces and aid workers lose count of the number of dead before all residents of opposition-held Aleppo were displaced to Idlib.

Even as UN investigators find Assad responsible for chemical attacks,[56] recent leaked UN documents[57] seem to suggest that the United Nations' reconstruction plans for the city have been heavily influenced by the Assad regime. Rebuilding the city Assad so wantonly destroyed under his direction will only further entrench the displacement of tens of thousands of its former residents.

This is hardly a surprise to those of us who have watched UN Syria operations closely, however. As one former UN official put it to the *Guardian*, every UN agency has hired at least "one person who is a direct relative of a Syrian official."[58]

THE CURRENT "DE-ESCALATION ZONES"

As of May 8, 2017, "de-escalation zones" are meant to be in effect in the four main opposition pockets left in Syria: Idlib Province and its environs, the Daraa and Quneitra provinces, the northern suburbs of Homs, and the East Ghouta suburbs of Damascus. These de-escalation zones were an outgrowth of the Astana diplomatic process that is jointly administered by Russia, Iran, and Turkey and is notable for its complete bypassing of any talk on a political transition. Trump Administration officials have spoken in favor of these zones, particularly after a de-escalation zone was announced for Daraa and

Quneitra soon after a meeting between Russian President Vladimir Putin and President Donald Trump.

The allure of these zones is that, temporarily at least, they have indeed reduced attacks by the Assad regime and its allies on many Syrian opposition population centers, particularly in Idlib, Daraa, and Homs. However, because these zones include no path to a nationwide transition plan and establish neither enforcement mechanisms nor linkages between different zones, the Russian "de-escalation zones" proposal essentially amounts to four large-scale local ceasefires, enacted simultaneously. This means that the zones are subject to the same abuses and revisions of terms found in previous "local ceasefires" signed by the regime.

Right from the beginning, the Assad regime and Russia have cloaked these zones in multiple layers of ambiguity. Russia announced de-escalation zones in four different regions of Syria, but then proceeded to negotiate separate agreements concerning the East Ghouta[59] and north Homs pockets,[60] with inferior terms for the opposition in each area. In an added layer of ambiguity, the East Ghouta ceasefire was undertaken only with the Jaish al-Islam rebel group, which provided a pretext for the regime to continue launching attacks[61] on territories in Ghouta controlled by the local Free Syrian Army branch. Similarly, although the ceasefire negotiated between Trump and Putin included the Syria-Israel border areas[62] in Quneitra Province, Russia later negotiated a separate deal with Jordan[63] covering only these border areas.

In addition to ambiguity on the details of these ceasefires, there is also an overarching ambiguity as to the overall purpose of the de-escalation zones. On the day the zones were announced, Russian officials explicitly framed the zones as helping Russian airmen to concentrate the fight on ISIS[64] in the Syrian desert. At the same time, the Assad regime's elite "Tiger Forces" militia redeployed from the northern Hama suburbs (adjoining the Idlib de-escalation zone) to the outskirts of the desert city of Palmyra.[65] The problem is that Assad regime forces began attacking not ISIS, but Pentagon-backed rebels who had been making rapid gains against ISIS[66] until then. The rebel forces were ultimately surrounded.

This regime behavior created a question concerning Russia and the regime's ultimate intentions behind the "de-escalation zones": were they meant as a permanent reduction in violence, perhaps in recognition that Assad could not conquer the remaining rebel areas? Or were they only meant as transient deals—like many previous local ceasefires in the Damascus suburbs—that would allow the regime to redeploy elsewhere before ultimately returning to attack the ceasefire areas with greater force?

Early on in the enactment of the "de-escalation zones," I warned American officials involved in the ceasefire process that the latter outcome was a distinct possibility. The regime has never fully ceased attacks on opposition areas since the start of the de-escalation zones. Quite the opposite; as the regime has conquered more territory in eastern Syria, protected its rear from attacks, and denied US-backed rebels a base, it has grown more confident and has gradually increased attacks on de-escalation zones. This effectively removed the zones from the ceasefire, in a strategy that had already been tried and tested in Madaya, Zabadani, Wadi Barada, Barzeh, and Waer.

First came the East Ghouta zone, in which regime attacks never really ceased, and where the regime gradually tightened its siege[67] since the de-escalation zone's enactment. The regime leveraged the Barzeh ceasefire, once called a "win-win-situation" by London School of Economics researchers, to tighten the siege because that ceasefire ultimately led to the regime's capture of Barzeh and the removal of a smuggling route to Ghouta outside regime control. The UN recently called the situation in East Ghouta a "humanitarian emergency" and declared "there is only escalation in this de-escalation zone."[68]

Next came the southwest Syrian zone and Idlib Province in September 2017, as Assad forces began new bombardments on the opposition-held Hermon Mountains in Quneitra and Russia resumed bombing Idlib in dramatic fashion by targeting multiple medical centers. Though the pace of Russian airstrikes on Idlib then decreased, regime offensives on both Quneitra and Idlib have continued from then on. Tellingly, the regime offensive on Idlib began in the eastern desert areas, to which regime units who had fought ISIS in the east were returning. The Idlib offensive therefore represents the regime parlaying its gains in the east into renewed attacks on Syria's most populated de-escalation zone.

CONCLUSION

At present, the Assad regime and its allies—with acquiescence from the international community and relying heavily on its "local ceasefires" strategy for systematic sectarian cleansing—is in a stronger military position than at any point since the start of armed conflict. Homs and Aleppo, two of the three largest cities in Syria, have risen and fallen as revolutionary centers amidst wholesale population displacement by Assad and his allies. Iconic revolutionary protest centers in highly strategic areas such as Darayya and Zabadani have seen their populations besieged, starved, and forcibly displaced. In many of these areas, displaced civilians have had their belongings looted and placed on sale at "Sunni markets" while highly sectarian policies concerning refugee returns and resettlement have been put in place.

Even if all fighting in Syria stopped tomorrow and the pre-Revolution veneer of "peace" returned to the land, the cities Assad conquered would remain deeply wounded and the refugees he displaced would still be uprooted from their homes. Assad himself has said this; in a speech to his parliament on July 26, 2015, he stated that "Syria is not for those who hold passports . . . but for those who defend it."[69] And as the Assad regime, Russia, and Iran's final bloody offensive on Aleppo was under way, Assad remarked, "You have to keep cleaning this area and to push the terrorists to Turkey[70] to go back to where they came from, or to kill them." Similarly, soon after regime troops reached the main eastern Syrian city of Deir Ezzor, the top regime general for eastern Syria, Issam Zahreddine, threatened, "To those who fled to other countries, I beg you don't ever return, because even if the government forgives you, we will never forgive or forget. If you know what is good for you, none of you return." Policymakers may have no interest in confronting Assad or his allies, but if they wish to solve the Syrian refugee crisis, they must grapple with the full implications of these statements.

The Assad regime's vision for a final "peace" in Syria is merely a scaled-up version of the "local ceasefires" and sectarian cleansing that has already taken place in many locales of Syria. Expert analyses advocating an "ink-blot" strategy and diplomatic UN initiatives for local "freeze zones" or—in the current parlance, as coined by Russian diplomats at the Astana talks— "de-escalation zones" play directly into the Assad regime's hands and will worsen sectarian displacement in the long run. The dire and worsening humanitarian conditions in East Ghouta are the clearest example of Assad's ultimate plan for "de-escalation zones."

With pro-Assad forces now gaining traction even in Idlib, the main opposition bastion that has served as the regime's demographic dumping ground for so long, it is only a matter of time before the pro-Assad alliance reaches major population centers in the province. Then, Assad forces will have a chance to make good on the regime's threat to "cleanse this area" and push its residents into Turkey, triggering a new refugee crisis of even greater proportions. Until then, there is still time for the international community to ensure the protection of civilians and a democratic transition based on increased opposition leverage rather than bogus peace deals.

NOTES

1. Holmes, Oliver, and Tom Miles. "Syrian Army Moves into Rebel-Free Homs, Starts De-Mining Operation." Reuters. May 09, 2014. https://www.reuters.com/article/us-syria-crisis-homs/syrian-army-moves-into-rebel-free-homs-starts-de-mining-operation-idUSBREA4806Q20140509.

2. Stevenson, Jonathan, and Steven Simon. "A New Plan for Syria." The New York Review of Books. http://www.nybooks.com/daily/2014/09/26/how-stabilize-syria/.

3. Sayigh, Yezid. "To Confront the Islamic State, Seek a Truce in Syria." Carnegie Middle East Center. http://carnegie-mec.org/2014/09/18/to-confront-islamic-state-seek-truce-in-syria.

4. Jenkins, Brian Michael. "The Dynamics of Syria's Civil War." RAND Corporation. January 17, 2014. https://www.rand.org/pubs/perspectives/PE115.html.

5. "The Syrian Regime's Military Solution to the War." The Syrian Regime's Military Solution to the War - The Washington Institute for Near East Policy. http://www.washingtoninstitute.org/policy-analysis/view/the-syrian-regimes-military-solution-to-the-war.

6. Al-Khalidi;, Suleiman. "Syrian, Russian Jets Bomb Residential Areas in Eastern Ghouta: Witness." Reuters. https://www.reuters.com/article/us-mideast-crisis-syria-ghouta/syrian-russian-jets-bomb-residential-areas-in-eastern-ghouta-witnesses-monitor-idUSKBN1DY01J.

7. Solomon, Erika, and Editing By Ralph Boulton. "In Syria's Homs, Sectarian Spoils of War at Bargain Prices." Reuters. June 19, 2012. https://www.reuters.com/article/us-syria-crisis-shopping/in-syrias-homs-sectarian-spoils-of-war-at-bargain-prices-idUSBRE85I0G020120619.

8. The Syria Institute and PAX. "No Return to Homs: A Case Study on Demographic Engineering in Syria." February 21, 2017. http://syriainstitute.org/2017/02/21/no-return-to-homs-a-case-study-on-demographic-engineering-in-syria/.

9. Associated Press. "Syria's Onetime 'Capital of the Revolution' Now a Ghost Town." Boston Herald. February 28, 2016. http://www.bostonherald.com/news/international/2016/02/syrias_onetime_capital_of_the_revolution_now_a_ghost_town.

10. "Research Summary Report: Local Truces and Ceasefires." Civil Society Knowledge Centre. March 16, 2017. http://civilsociety-centre.org/resource/research-summary-report-local-truces-and-ceasefires.

11. Eid, Kassem. "I Survived a Sarin Gas Attack." The New York Times. April 07, 2017. https://www.nytimes.com/2017/04/07/opinion/what-its-like-to-survive-a-sarin-gas-attack.html.

12. ZAMAN ALWSL. "Hundreds Evacuated from Besieged Camp of Yarmouk." February 02, 2014. https://en.zamanalwsl.net/news/3511.html.

13. Al Jazeera. May 07, 2017. http://bit.ly/2j9weJa.

14. ZAMAN ALWSL. "Damascus: Efforts Intensify to Break Siege of Southern Suburbs."Feb 22, 2015. https://en.zamanalwsl.net/news/9090.html.

15. Ghanem, Mohammed Alaa. "The Nail in the Coffin for 'Local Ceasefires' in Syria." The Hill. April 20, 2015. http://thehill.com/blogs/congress-blog/foreign-policy/239169-the-nail-in-the-coffin-for-local-ceasefires-in-syria.

16. Barnard, Anne. "Residents Abandon Daraya as Government Seizes a Symbol of Syria's Rebellion." The New York Times. August 26, 2016 https://www.nytimes.com/2016/08/27/world/middleeast/syria-daraya-falls-symbol-rebellion.html.

17. Rim Turkmani, Mary Kaldor, Wisam Elhamwi, Joan Ayo, and Nael Hariri. "Hungry for Peace: Positives and Drawbacks of Local Truces and Ceasefires in Syria." Nov 2014 http://www.lse.ac.uk/website-archive/newsAndMedia/news/archives/2014/11/Syriareport.aspx.

18. Ghanem, Mohammed Alaa. "The U.N is Walking into a Trap in Syria—Here's How to Avoid It." The Huffington Post. November 24, 2014. http://www.huffingtonpost.com/mohammed-alaa-ghanem/the-un-is-walking-into-a-_b_6194760.html.

19. Dlewati, Hiba. "Years-Long Truces End As Government Tightens Control on Damascus." Syria. May 19, 2017. https://www.newsdeeply.com/syria/articles/2017/05/18/syria-its-not-a-truce-until-government-tanks-are-in-the-square.

20. "Syria Conflict: Rebels Leave Homs Under Truce." BBC News. December 09, 2015. http://www.bbc.com/news/world-middle-east-35048404.

21. "Rebels Leave Al Waer District Under Evacuation Deal." Syria News | Al Jazeera. March 18, 2017. http://www.aljazeera.com/news/2017/03/rebels-leave-al-waer-district-evacuation-deal-170318094703849.html.

22. "Wadi Barada Uses Water Spring to Keep Regime Invasion at Bay." Syria Direct. November 20, 2013 http://syriadirect.org/news/wadi-barada-uses-water-spring-to-keep-regime-invasion-at-bay/.

23. "Al-Qalamoun, Wadi Barada, Al-Damar Al-Hasel Fi Naba'a Ain al-Feijeh." YouTube. December 27, 2016. https://www.youtube.com/watch?v=ABEFRxSVpbE.

24. Ghanem, Mohammed Alaa. "Assad's Newest War Tactic: Dehydration." The Daily Beast. January 05, 2017. https://www.thedailybeast.com/assads-newest-war-tactic-dehydration.

25. Ensor, Josie. "Syrian Rebels Evacuated out of Besieged Wadi Barada After Government Forces Capture Strategic Water Spring." The Telegraph. January 30, 2017. http://www.

telegraph.co.uk/news/2017/01/30/syrian-rebels-evacuated-besieged-wadi-barada-government-forces/.

26. "Syria Conflict: 'Unprecedented' Assault on Zabadani." BBC News. July 22, 2015. http://www.bbc.com/news/world-middle-east-33624215.

27. "Syrian Army and Hezbollah on the Edge of Downtown Al-Zabadani." AMN - Al-Masdar News. July 14, 2015. https://www.almasdarnews.com/article/syrian-army-and-hezbollah-on-the-edge-of-downtown-al-zabadani/.

28. "Hathi Hya Bunood Ittifaq al-Zabadani-Al-Foua-Kafreya." Al-Hadath News. September 27, 2015. http://www.alhadathnews.net/archives/165130.

29. Asher-Schapiro, Avi. "'Children Are Eating Leaves off the Trees': The Nightmare of the Siege of Madaya, Syria." VICE News. January 04, 2016. https://news.vice.com/article/children-are-eating-leaves-off-the-trees-the-nightmare-of-the-siege-of-madaya-syria.

30. Barnard, Anne. "As Rebel-Held Town of Madaya Starves, Syria Agrees to Food Aid, U.N. Says." The New York Times. January 07, 2016. http://www.nytimes.com/2016/01/08/world/middleeast/madaya-syria-starvation.html?_r=0.

31. Sami. "#Syria 5 yr old Hussain Tinawi in #Madaya was shot in the jaw by #Hezbollah snipers, needs urgent medical attention pic.twitter.com/ly0BDS4j9D." Twitter. August 29, 2016. https://twitter.com/paradoxy13/status/770278894763147264.

32. "Mother of 9-Year-Old Girl Targeted by a Sniper's Bullet Calls for Evacuation from Madaya: 'She Is in Urgent Need of Trauma Surgery'." Syria Direct. August 10, 2016. http://syriadirect.org/news/mother-of-9-year-old-girl-targeted-by-a-sniper%E2%80%99s-bullet-calls-for-evacuation-from-madaya-%E2%80%98she-is-in-urgent-need-of-trauma-surgery%E2%80%99/.

33. "Increase in Child Suicide Attempts in Madaya as Sieges worsen across Syria." Save the Children International. September 07, 2016. https://www.savethechildren.net/article/increase-child-suicide-attempts-madaya-sieges-worsen-across-syria.

34. Ensor, Josie. "Evacuation Deal Reached for Four Besieged Syrian Towns Where Civilians are Trapped in 'Catastrophic' Conditions." The Telegraph. March 29, 2017. http://www.telegraph.co.uk/news/2017/03/29/evacuation-deal-reached-four-besieged-syrian-towns-civilians/.

35. Clarke, Hilary. "Thousands Evacuate Besieged Syrian Towns." CNN. April 14, 2017. http://www.cnn.com/2017/04/14/middleeast/syria-evacuations/index.html.

36. "Security Council Endorses Syria Cessation of Hostilities Accord, Unanimously Adopting Resolution 2268 (2016) | Meetings Coverage and Press Releases." United Nations. https://www.un.org/press/en/2016/sc12261.doc.htm.

37. "John Kerry Secretary of State: Joint Press Availability With Russian Foreign Minister Sergey Lavrov and UN Special Envoy Staffan de Mistura, 17 May 2016." ReliefWeb. http://reliefweb.int/report/syrian-arab-republic/john-kerry-secretary-state-joint-press-availability-russian-foreign.

38. Zakarya, Qusai. "Hunger Strike Under Siege: Moadamiya, Syria on WordPress.com." December 06, 2013. https://stopthesiege.wordpress.com/page/4/.

39. Barnard, Anne, and Saad, Hwaida. "Stark Choice for Syrians in Rebel Areas: 'Doom' or the Green Bus." The New York Times, 29 Oct. 2016, www.nytimes.com/2016/10/30/world/middleeast/once-propelled-by-hope-for-a-modern-syria-green-buses-now-run-on-tears.html.

40. "Report of the Secretary-General on the implementation of Security Council resolutions 2139 (2014), 2165 (2014) and 2191 (2014)." United Nations Security Council. December 11, 2015.

41. "'Two Years Under Siege, and It Wnds with Displacement'." Syria News | Al Jazeera. April 14, 2017. http://www.aljazeera.com/news/2017/04/exchange-residents-begins-evacuation-deal-170414051642212.html.

42. "Joint Statement on Hard-to-Reach and Besieged Communities in Syria [EN/AR]." ReliefWeb. January 07, 2016. http://reliefweb.int/report/syrian-arab-republic/join-statement-hard-reach-and-besieged-communities-syria-enar.

43. Gutman, Roy. "How the U.N. Let Assad Edit the Truth of Syria's War." Foreign Policy. January 27, 2016. http://foreignpolicy.com/2016/01/27/syria-madaya-starvation-united-nations-humanitarian-response-plan-assad-edited/.

44. Abdulrahim, Raja. "Aleppo, Syria, Could Soon Be Under Siege by Government Troops." Los Angeles Times. November 23, 2014. http://www.latimes.com/world/middleeast/la-fg-syria-aleppo-siege-20141123-story.html.

45. Chulov, Martin. "Syrian Rebels Prepare to Defend Ruined Aleppo as Troops and Militias Close In." The Guardian. December 23, 2014. https://www.theguardian.com/world/2014/dec/23/syria-battle-for-aleppo.

46. Doucet, Lyse. "Could Aleppo Plan Cut Syrian Bloodshed?" BBC News. December 15, 2014. http://www.bbc.com/news/world-asia-30476378.

47. "UN Envoy Proposes Syria 'Fighting Freeze'." Al Jazeera News. October 31, 2014. http://www.aljazeera.com/news/middleeast/2014/10/un-envoy-proposes-syria-fighting-freeze-201410316401831395.html.

48. Ghanem, Mohammed Alaa. "The U.N Is Walking into a Trap in Syria—Here's How to Avoid It." The Huffington Post. November 24, 2014. http://www.huffingtonpost.com/mohammed-alaa-ghanem/the-un-is-walking-into-a-_b_6194760.html.

49. Sengupta, Somini, and Barnard, Anne. "U.N. Envoy to Syria Announces Possible Truce in Aleppo." The New York Times. February 17, 2015. http://www.nytimes.com/2015/02/18/world/middleeast/syrian-forces-try-to-cut-supply-route-to-aleppo-as-hezbollahs-role-grows.html?_r=0.

50. Shaheen, Kareem. "Aleppo Ceasefire Plan in Danger as Assad's Troops Fail to Close Off City." The Guardian. February 20, 2015. http://www.theguardian.com/world/2015/feb/20/aleppo-ceasefire-assad-un.

51. Laura Pitel, Kim Sengupta. "Syria Civil War: President Assad's Forces Cut Off Last Rebel Supply Line to Aleppo Raising Fears of Huge Humanitarian Crisis." The Independent. February 03, 2016. http://www.independent.co.uk/news/world/middle-east/syria-civil-war-assad-s-forces-cut-off-last-rebel-supply-line-to-aleppo-raising-fears-of-huge-a6851776.html.

52. "Syria's War: Calls for Truce to Get Aid into Aleppo." Al Jazeera. August 22, 2016. http://www.aljazeera.com/news/2016/08/syria-war-calls-truce-aid-aleppo-160821052204413.html.

53. "Aid Convoys 'Ready' to Enter Aleppo; UN Envoys Await Russia-US Talks on Truce." UN News Center. August 25, 2016. http://www.un.org/apps/news/story.asp?NewsID=54758#.WVOcscaZPBK.

54. "Which Road to Aleppo? Opposition Refuses Aid Delivery via Castello Road." Syria Direct. http://syriadirect.org/news/which-road-to-aleppo-opposition-refuses-aid-delivery-via-castello-road/.

55. Michael Weiss, Roy Gutman, and Alex Rowell. "Women in Aleppo Choose Suicide Over Rape, Rebels Report." The Daily Beast. December 13, 2016. https://www.thedailybeast.com/women-in-aleppo-choose-suicide-over-rape-rebels-report.

56. Gladstone, Rick. "U.N. Panel Points Finger at Syria in Sarin Attack on Village." The New York Times. October 26, 2017. https://www.nytimes.com/2017/10/26/world/middleeast/syria-chemical-khan-shekhoun.html.

57. "UN Allowing Assad Government to Take Lead in Rebuilding Aleppo." Fox News. http://www.foxnews.com/world/2017/11/16/un-allowing-assad-government-to-take-lead-in-rebuilding-aleppo.html.

58. Hopkins, Nick, and Emma Beals. "UN Hires Assad's Friends and Relatives for Syria Relief Operation." The Guardian. October 28, 2016. Accessed December 18, 2017. https://www.theguardian.com/world/2016/oct/28/un-hires-assads-friends-and-relatives-for-syria-relief-operation.

59. "Russia: New Ceasefire Deal Agreed in Syria's Ghouta." Syria News | Al Jazeera. July 22, 2017. http://www.aljazeera.com/news/2017/07/russia-ceasefire-deal-agreed-syria-ghouta-170722215635284.html.

60. Mourad, Mahmoud, Maria Kiselyova, and Dmitry Solovyov. "Russia Announces 'De-Escalation Zone' North of Syria's City of Homs." Reuters. August 03, 2017. https://www.reuters.com/article/us-mideast-crisis-syria-russia/russia-announces-de-escalation-zone-north-of-syrias-city-of-homs-idUSKBN1AJ0S6.

61. "Russia Muscles in on De-Escalation Zones." Syria From Within, Chatham House. October 2017. https://syria.chathamhouse.org/research/russia-muscles-in-on-de-escalation-zones.

62. Josh Lederman, Vivian Salama, and Ken Thomas. "US, Russia Announce Syria Cease-Fire after Trump-Putin Talks." AP News. July 08, 2017. https://www.apnews.com/eaa310ccb6e04e0580759d4ce36e778b.

63. Al-Khalidi;, Suleiman. "Russia, Jordan Agree to Speed De-Escalation Aone in South Syria." Reuters. September 11, 2017. https://www.reuters.com/article/us-mideast-crisis-jordan-russia/russia-jordan-agree-to-speed-de-escalation-zone-in-south-syria-idUSKCN1BM2A5.

64. "Syria De-Escalation Zones Go into Effect at Midnight - General news - ANSAMed." May 08, 2017. http://www.ansamed.info/ansamed/en/news/sections/generalnews/2017/05/05/syria-de-escalation-zones-go-into-effect-at-midnight_50f742b2-50d8-4c80-b294-37965532aa51.html.

65. "Exclusive: Tiger Forces Deploy to Palmyra Front for Massive Offensive." AMN - Al-Masdar News . May 05, 2017. https://www.almasdarnews.com/article/exclusive-tiger-forces-deploy-palmyra-front-massive-offensive/.

66. "E. #Qalamoun: #FSA seized over several defensive positions from #ISIS around #Muhassah (red). Clashes ongoing. Qalaat Al Mudiq. pic.twitter.com/sH0JdxSexh." Twitter. April 23, 2017. https://twitter.com/QalaatAlMudiq/status/856217635297669121.

67. "Syrian Regime Traps 400,000 Civilians in East Ghouta." Al Jazeera. October 23, 2017. http://www.aljazeera.com/news/2017/10/syrian-regime-traps-400000-civilians-east-ghouta-171023072533308.html.

68. Nebehay, Stephanie . "U.N. Seeks Urgent Medical Evacuation of 500 from Syria's Eastern Ghouta." Reuters. November 30, 2017. https://www.reuters.com/article/us-mideast-crisis-syria-aid/u-n-seeks-urgent-medical-evacuation-of-500-from-syrias-eastern-ghouta-idUSKBN1DU1OK.

69. "Speech by Bashar al-Assad" YouTube. July 26, 2015. https://www.youtube.com/watch?v=z5Gznln1LHY.

70. "Aleppo Must Be 'Cleaned', Declares Assad, Amid Outcry Over Bloody Siege." The Guardian. October 13, 2016. https://www.theguardian.com/world/2016/oct/14/aleppo-must-be-cleaned-declares-assad-amid-outcry-over-bloody-siege.

Chapter Seven

The Promises and Pitfalls of Data Analysis for Accountability and Justice

Megan Price and Anita Gohdes

Transitional justice mechanisms rely on an accurate accounting of what happened during a conflict. Empirical evidence, including quantitative analyses, can contribute to establishing an accurate historical record. Correctly applied, rigorous analyses can both confirm and contextualize individual victim and witness accounts, as they did in the 2013 trial of Ríos Montt in Guatemala. Statistical analyses conducted by the Human Rights Data Analysis Group (HRDAG) found that members of the indigenous Mayan population were five to eight times more likely to be killed by the army than their non-indigenous neighbors. Along with other evidence, the judges found this to be consistent with the charges of genocide. In their guilty verdict, the judges stated that the statistical evidence confirmed, "in numerical form, what the victims said."[1]

This is the goal of quantitative analyses of mass violence—to confirm, contextualize, and amplify the stories of victims and witnesses. To do so, statistical analyses must provide an accurate account of events. They must be appropriate for the data available and suitable to answer the substantive questions of interest. When they are not, when statistical analyses risk being insufficiently rigorous to withstand the adversarial environment of a courtroom or politicized debate, they can weaken and distract from advocacy efforts.

Since 2012 we have been working with multiple Syrian documentation groups to better understand the violent evolution of conflict in their country. During that time, we have also partnered with the United Nations Office of the High Commissioner for Human Rights to publish reports describing documented, identified victims, and Amnesty International on estimating the number of victims who were killed specifically while in custody. Our contributions to establishing death tolls in Syria have only been possible due to the tireless and detail-oriented work by multiple documentation groups.

Over the course of the conflict we have worked with a number of groups, including the Center for Research and Statistics in Syria, the Damascus Center for Human Rights Science, the Syrian Network for Human Rights, and the Violations Documentation Center. All of the groups we have worked with are collecting data on individual victims of lethal violence. For each victim, the groups report a number of covariates, including the name, the date of death, the location of death, as well as civilian status, age, and the circumstances and cause of death.

We do not yet know specifically what accountability mechanisms will be implemented in Syria, nor what questions they will raise. But as a starting point, any historical record will have to determine how many people have been killed. As Hagan et al. point out, "The structure of international criminal law . . . holds to the dictum 'no body, no crime.' This presents significant problems for lawyers investigating or prosecuting heads of state for crimes against humanity that can be hidden behind the doctrine of state autonomy. To establish legal responsibility, either bodies must be uncovered from mass graves and identified, as was done in Srebrenica, or the number of deaths must be otherwise convincingly established."[2]

As Hagan et al. imply, convincingly establishing the number of deaths must involve more than simply recording known victims. This is a crucial first step, but it is an insufficient stopping point since it fails to account for unknown, unidentified victims. Statistical tools exist for estimating what we do not know, and they must be applied to analytical efforts for establishing accountability and justice.

In this chapter, we present the limitations of observed data, briefly discuss statistical methods for estimating what has not been observed, and present two specific challenges to data analysis of human rights violations in the Syrian conflict, namely the complexities surrounding the identification of multiple (or duplicate) records, and the challenges of recording fatalities during ongoing hostilities.

DATA ANALYSIS FOR ACCOUNTABILITY

In conflict and other violent settings, information about human rights violations is often collected by various actors on the ground. The form of this information varies, and since the development of social media platforms we have seen an increase in digital record collection. The types of record-keeping vary widely, including hand-written names of victims, YouTube videos of violent acts, spreadsheets with details of incidences, or testimonies collected by a truth commission (among many other examples). All of this information is valuable, but to contribute to accountability it is crucial that we ask both *why* and *how* the information was collected, and that the answers to these questions is taken into account in analyses and interpretations.

Identifying patterns requires statistics

Individuals, groups, and organizations collecting information on violent events may have different motivations to do so. Information about individual cases may be collected to honor and memorialize the victims. It may also be collected to provide substantive evidence about the types of violations that occurred, even if the information only includes part of what happened.

These cases may form the basis for future investigations, or may themselves provide sufficient information to hold individual perpetrators accountable.

In other instances, the goal may be to answer more exhaustive questions about what happened: How many people were killed or disappeared overall? What were the most violent time periods and regions? Were specific ethnic or religious groups targeted more than others? Were some parts of the country disproportionately affected by the violence? These questions often lead to more specific investigations about patterns of violence that would support specific charges of crimes. For example, violations may be described as "systematic," "widespread," or "targeted." While these concepts oftentimes have clear legal definitions, they also have important implications for the type of evidence and analysis required to investigate them.

Rigorous statistical analyses can contribute to these investigations, but to do so they must account for the ways in which the underlying data were generated or collected.

Accounting for unobserved violence

In the vast majority of instances of mass violence, documenting information on the victims of said violence is very difficult, and usually incomplete. In other words, it is usually only possible to collect information on a subset of the total number of victims. In most cases, there remain an unknown number of unidentified, undocumented victims. To establish the kinds of patterns and comparisons described above, analyses must account for this incompleteness. Analyses that fail to account for unobserved data will be insufficient to answer substantive questions of interest.

In our experience, descriptive analyses of observed records do not simply underestimate violence, they run the risk of drawing completely incorrect conclusions about patterns of violence. In this section, we discuss the difference between observed and unobserved violence, and how unobserved violence needs to be statistically accounted for in analyses that seek to make claims about patterns of dynamics of violence. We then offer an example of such analysis from Syria, looking at fatalities in Hama in December 2012 and January 2013.

When we aim to identify patterns of violence, we have to make some important assumptions about the properties of the data we are using. The assumptions are that either (1) every single violation was observed, recorded, and is included in our data or (2) all violations that were not documented (and are thus unobserved) are represented, in a statistical sense, by the observed violations. In other words, that unobserved violations do not differ systematically from observed violations.

Both assumptions mentioned above are difficult to test, and they are rarely explicitly addressed in descriptive analyses of observed records. They are also rarely met in human rights research (and many other settings). In our experience, most analysts readily admit that some violations are unobserved. It is important to note that incomplete data do not imply low-quality data or a failure on the part of individuals or groups collecting data. Many (most) high-quality, systematic data collection efforts produce incomplete datasets.

This is the case in Syria, where we have been consistently impressed by the speed and attention to detail carried out by the numerous groups documenting violations in the ongoing conflict. Nonetheless, these records can only account for a subset of all victims. The documentation groups do an excellent job of being transparent about the challenges and limitations of their work.

For example, a report from the Syrian Network for Human Rights (SNHR) describing the number of civilian victims documented in August 2017[3] includes the following paragraphs:

> Furthermore, the report notes that SNHR team encounters difficulties in documenting victims from armed opposition factions as many of those victims are killed on battlefronts and not inside cities. Also, we aren't able to obtain details such as names, pictures and other important details on account of the armed opposition forces' unwillingness to reveal such information for security concerns among other reasons. Therefore, the actual number of victims is much greater than what is being recorded.
>
> On the other side, the report stresses that it is almost impossible to access information about victims from Syrian regime forces or from ISIS and the margin of error is considerably higher due to the lack of any applicable methodology in this type of documentation. The Syrian government and ISIS don't publish, reveal, or record their victims.

As another example, in their report "Stolen Futures: The Hidden Toll of Child Casualties in Syria"[4] the Oxford Research Group (ORG) conducted a survey of four documentation groups. As part of that survey they asked about challenges to data collection and reported the following:

> Achieving comprehensive coverage of all areas remains a key challenge for any single organization, and not only from the dangers posed to field workers. Although all organizations claim to cover all regions and districts of Syria, VDC [Violations Documentation Center] and ST [Syria Tracker] state that obtaining information on casualties in areas now under opposition control is impeded by electricity shortages and lack of Internet connectivity. ST also noted that in some parts of Syria there is less awareness among citizens of the value of systematically reporting casualties, leading to ST receiving fewer reports and data from those areas.

Additionally:

> As with information collection, systematic verification of information be-comes increasingly difficult as the conflict intensifies. In addition, in some areas witnesses and the families of victims fear reprisal attacks and so refuse to share details of casualties.

This is a reality of collecting data on violent conflict—it is (generally) not possible to collect information about every victim. What's important is that analyses and interpretations appropriately account for unobserved data. It is most often at the stage of analysis that conclusions about "on-the-ground" realities are drawn that are not compatible with the realities of reporting.

The challenges described above will inevitably result in a different pro-portion of victims being documented at different times, in different geo-graphic regions, and for different victim and perpetrator characteristics. Therefore, comparisons along any of these categories must adjust for this variable coverage rate. The technical term for this variable coverage rate is *bias*. Comparisons that ignore such *bias* inevitably conflate reporting rates with incidence rates, and thus risk drawing the wrong conclusions.

This is related to the second assumption described above, which is subtler and often more difficult to address. As a hypothetical example, suppose we wanted to analyze whether ethnic group A was targeted by violence more frequently than ethnic group B. If we had the same proportion of information (i.e., the same coverage) for both ethnic groups, this comparison would be straightforward. But we cannot conclude, from the observed data *alone*, what proportion of information we have observed. If we recorded more informa-tion for group A than for group B, we might conclude that group A was targeted more frequently, merely because we have more information on the egregious crimes committed against them. Put differently, the fact that we have a higher proportion of *unobserved* violence for group B means that we learn less about their fate, and thus may draw entirely wrong conclusions about who was targeted during the period of mass violence.

As the example of ethnic groups A and B suggests, small differences in the amount of information available may have grave consequences for the conclusions we draw about who was most affected by violence. Differences in the level of coverage for different groups (or regions, or time periods, etc.), as described qualitatively in the preceding quotes from SNHR and ORG, are difficult to detect and asses quantitatively, and require appropriate analytical methods. As such, acknowledging incompleteness of data but then proceeding with analyses of the data as if they were either complete or representative renders the analysis insufficient for the purposes of establishing accountability and justice.

There are a number of statistical methods appropriate for analyzing incomplete data; which method is suitable for a given situation depends on the ways in which the data are incomplete, how the data were collected, and what other data may be available. For example, if the data were collected using a probabilistic selection method, such as a household survey, then we can use appropriate methods to determine how those who were included in the survey represent those who were not surveyed.[5]

If data were not collected in a way that allows us to infer what part of the population each data point is representing, the sample is referred to as a convenience sample. This does not imply the sample was convenient to collect—as is certainly the case in Syria (and many other conflict situations), quite the opposite is true. The important feature of a convenience sample is the fact that it includes an *unknown* subset of the underlying population of interest. For example, we currently do not know how many unidentified victims have been killed in Syria, and as a result, we do not know how many victims each recorded, identified victim must represent. For example, a convenience sample of fatalities in Syria may in one month cover 70 percent of all victims in one governorate, but only 45 percent in another governorate. In the following month, it may cover 60 percent and 50 percent of all fatalities in the same governorates. The unknown subset of those killed in the conflict thus varies, and is, as the name implies, not known to us. However, there are other statistical tools that can be used to extrapolate from convenience samples to draw appropriate conclusions about the population. One of these methods is multiple systems estimation (MSE), which we rely on in a variety of projects to analyze convenience sample data.

To illustrate our argument, let's consider an analysis we conducted of violence perpetrated in the governorate of Hama in December 2012 and January 2013.[6] We show that data combined from four different sources report very similar levels of violence for both December and January. However, we find that the *structure* of the data is very different for these two months: in December, the overlap of information (those victims who were reported by more than one source) is quite large, while it is smaller in January. When we estimate the *unknown* number of victims—those who were not documented by *any* of the groups—we find a far higher number in January than December. So, while the observed data reports similar levels of violence for the two consecutive months, the statistics reveal a high level of *unobserved* violence in January. We would have missed this spike in violence if we had not made use of appropriate methods to correct for changes in reporting. There are many reasons why levels of reporting change across time, some of which are directly related to the severity of violence happening on the ground. During particularly intense periods of fighting, the documentation of victims may become too dangerous. As described in the examples from SNHR and ORG, there are many other factors that influence reporting rates as well, including changes in perpetrators, territorial control, resources, and infrastructure.

This example shows how easy it can be to conflate *reports* of violence with *incidences* of violence. Drawing conclusions about patterns of observed violence is tempting, but we must always first consider the mechanism by which the information we are evaluating was collected and what might be missing from that information. Only then can we do our best to account for unobserved violence in our analyses and interpretations.

Identifying duplicate records

The finding described above is the result of a multi-step analysis involving two broad classes of methods—record linkage and multiple systems estimation (MSE). Fully describing either method is beyond the scope of this chapter, but we do want to highlight a small piece of the work identifying multiple records that refer to the same victim. In other words, determining the structure of the data, specifically the size of the "overlap" across datasets as mentioned in the previous section.

The groups documenting victims in Syria rely on networks of individuals to collect and verify information. Since some of these networks may rely on the same sources for verification, or the networks themselves may overlap, the same fatality may be documented by more than one group. Some fatalities may also be documented by the same group more than once because different informants may collect information on the same person. These multiple records that represent the same victim make it possible to employ statistical techniques to better understand a more complete picture of the violence occurring in Syria. To be clear, this is an important and useful feature of the data collected by these groups.

What this means is that one of the first steps in our analysis is to identify the multiple (or duplicated) records both *within* each individual group's database, and *across* the different groups' databases. Since the 1990s our team has specialized in implementing computer science methods for this process, which are conventionally known as record linkage methods. These methods have evolved over the years, and the challenges and limitations to applying them are context-specific. For example, the density of information varies across contexts. Sometimes all we have is a name and possible year of death to work with, while in other cases—such as Syria—more granular data is available.[7]

In short, we rely on a combination of human review and computer modeling to identify multiple records that refer to the same victim. A person (or several people) reviews a subset of records and identifies groups of records that they believe refer to the same individual. This information is then used to "teach" a computer model to identify attributes shared by records that are likely to refer to the same victim. The computer model then suggests other groups of records that may refer to the same individual. These groups are again reviewed by human coders. This process is iterated and a variety of metrics are evaluated. Again, this is a very simplified description of a complicated, multi-step process.[8]

One of the key pieces of information that we use to identify multiple records is the victim's name. For this reason, the complexities of names, and naming conventions that are specific to individual cultures, languages, religions, and political contexts have a significant impact on our record linkage procedure. As an example, in many Latin American countries naming conventions include both the father's and mother's name, which results in individuals carrying a number of different names, which they may or may not fully use in all social contexts. In some conflicts, combatants may take on a "Nom de guerre," and consequently their identity may be reported as either the nom de guerre, their birth name, or a combination of the two.

The intensity and geographic concentration of violence in Syria, combined with the fact that a handful of Arabic Syrian names are very commonly used, means that the data we have access to include records with very similar names and identical places and dates of death. These might represent multiple records describing the same individual, they might represent members of the same family who were all killed on the same day, or some combination. Table 1 includes a specific example of six records describing someone(s) killed in Rural Damascus in 2013. We think these six records most likely describe two individuals, probably a father and son. However, given how common the names involved are, it is possible that we are mistaken.

Conventional matching approaches work under the assumption that we can definitively determine whether two or more records refer to the same person based on the covariate information available for each record. The example above suggests that this assumption may not always hold when victims have very similar names and when the intensity of violence leads to a large number of victims documented at very similar times and locations. An

Table 7.1.   Example of records of victims

Name	Sex	DOD	Governorate
MOHAMMED HAMAD	M	24/03/13	Rural Damascus
MOHAMMED HAMAD	M	24/03/13	Rural Damascus
MOHAMMED HAMAD	M	24/03/13	Rural Damascus
SAMER MOHAMMED HAMAD	M	24/03/13	Rural Damascus
SAMI MOHAMMED HAMAD	M	24/03/13	Rural Damascus
SAMI MOHAMMED HAMAD	M	24/03/13	Rural Damascus

approach is therefore needed that takes the uncertainty about matching decisions—as illustrated in the table above—into account.

We have introduced a new approach, which we refer to as *probabilistic matching*. Probabilistic matching provides a way for human reviewers to explicitly provide information about their uncertainty regarding potential matching records by assigning a subjective probability to multiple possible groupings of records. For example, a human reviewer may be fairly confident that the above cluster of records represents two individuals, but they may think there is a small chance that this group of records represents a single individual or possibly three different individuals. The reviewer could express this by assigning an 80 percent probability to dividing the records into two groups (representing two individuals), with a 10 percent probability assigned to a single group (all records referring to the same victim), and the remaining 10 percent to three groups (three different individuals). Thus, instead of providing the computer model with definitive decisions on how to group the records in this cluster, we are providing it a probabilistic assessment that takes into account the uncertainty the human reviewer is expressing over the information at hand. This uncertainty is crucial to the construction of the computer-based matching model, as it allows us to understand how minor changes in matching decisions may affect our overall number of records. It also allows us to carry through this uncertainty in the final step of our analysis, the statistical models used to estimate the total number of victims, including those *not* documented by any of the groups.

We should note that this complexity and uncertainty exists for records of fully identified individual victims. The case is even more difficult (virtually impossible) for anonymous victims. For example, if one source describes five victims, and another seven victims, but neither identifies individual victims, we have no way of determining which (if any) of the same individuals were reported by both sources. For each event, we can bound the possible number of victims: if every victim reported in the first source was included in the report from the second source, then we can assume there were seven victims. At the other extreme, if none of the victims reported in the first source were included in the second, then we should conclude that there were 12 total victims. But it is equally possible that the truth is somewhere in between—that some, but not all, of the victims from the first source were also reported in the second, in which case perhaps the true total number of victims is somewhere between 6 and 11.

The problem is that without additional information we have no way of knowing which scenario is correct. And, therefore, we have no way of comparing that report of victims to any other and drawing conclusions about whether the number of victims was higher or lower following a certain event or in a certain place or at a certain time. This is the limitation of aggregated counts of victims—they tell an important story about a specific event, but they are insufficient inputs to analyses meant to draw conclusions about patterns of violence (over time, geographic region, or the characteristics of victims or perpetrators).

CONCLUSION

Counting casualties seems straightforward, but it involves a surprising amount of uncertainty. Even determining what we know can be difficult, as illustrated by the challenge of determining how many unique victims are described by a set of similar records. Once that has been accomplished we must then estimate what we don't know, what has not yet been observed and recorded. These challenges aren't meant to discourage the use of data analysis for justice and accountability, rather to highlight that there are methodological solutions to each of these challenges, and we owe it to the victims, witnesses, and data collectors to do the best work possible so that it furthers, rather than hinders, the pursuit of truth, justice, and accountability.

Quantitative analyses of human rights violations, not just fatalities, can help to establish a historical record and answer questions about patterns of violence. Such an approach has a lot of potential in the case of Syria, where large amounts of data have been and continue to be collected. But this data must be analyzed and interpreted correctly, or we risk weakening advocacy efforts. The challenges outlined in the previous sections, among others, must be addressed, or we risk leaving ourselves and our partners vulnerable to critiques. When we stand on the side of human rights, truth, and justice, we should not provide our adversaries the opportunity to accurately identify a methodological or technical weakness in our work.

NOTES

1. Translation provided by Patrick Ball. A link to the complete opinion, in Spanish, is available via HRDAG's website: https://hrdag.org/hat-tip-from-guatemala-judges/.

2. John Hagan, Heather Schoenfeld, and Alberto Palloni, "The Science of Human Rights, War Crimes, and Humanitarian Emergencies," *Annual Review of Sociology* 32 (2006): 329–349. We should note that as statisticians and social scientists we will not be addressing the potential legal intricacies of transitional justice and accountability in Syria. We will be focusing on the challenges of establishing systematic empirical evidence.

3. SNHR monthly report, http://sn4hr.org/blog/2017/09/04/46156/, accessed November 28, 2017.

4. Hamit Dardagan and Hana Salama, "Stolen Futures: The Hidden Toll of Child Casualties in Syria," November 2013.

5. In a household survey where the households were selected through a probabilistic selection method, the probability of selection can be used to calculate "weights" for each element (event, victim, household, etc.) in the sample. These weights then indicate how many *unobserved* elements each *observed* element represents (see, for example, Sergey Dorofeev and Peter Grant, *Statistics for Real-Life Sample Surveys: Non-Simple-Random Samples and Weighted Data* (New York: Cambridge University Press).

6. Megan Price, Anita Gohdes, and Patrick Ball, "Documents of War: Understanding the Syrian Conflict," Significance 12, no. 2 (April 2015): 17.

7. For descriptions of our evolving methodological approach to this problem, see Megan Price, Anita Gohdes, and Patrick Ball, "Technical Memo for Amnesty International Report on Deaths in Detention," August 18, 2016; Megan Price, Jeff Klingner, Anas Qtiesh, and Patrick Ball, "Updated Statistical Analysis of Documentation of Killings in the Syrian Arab Republic," June 13, 2013; and a series of blogposts on "Database Deduplication" here: https://hrdag.org/tech-corner/.

8. For a more technical description, see Megan Price, Anita Gohdes, and Patrick Ball, "Technical Memo for Amnesty International Report on Deaths in Detention," August 18, 2016, and a series of blogposts on "Database Deduplication" here: https://hrdag.org/tech-corner/.

Index

Additional Protocol I, 59
Additional Protocol II (AP II), 83; Article 1 of, 56, 57, 60; Article 17 of, 60–61
Afghanistan civil war, 12
aid: convoys blocked, 4, 30, 58, 74, 78, 80, 95, 96, 98, 99; Russia providing Assad, 5, 6–7, 31, 42n12, 55, 72, 81; UN demand and, 16, 17, 41n3, 45n42, 101; UN lack on, 30, 99, 100, 101; workers targeted, 81
air force: Afghanistan civil war using, 12; Chechnya civil war using, 12, 42n12; Darayya and attacks by, 80; government using, 12–14, 42n9; Somalia civil war using, 12, 42n11; al-Waer strikes by, 29. *See also* barrel bombs
Alawites: in army, intelligence services, 21; Homs city with increased, 79; increase in, 34; as pro-regime, 34; Sunni belongings sold by, 93; Sunnis counter protested by, 22–24, 26
Aleppo. *See* eastern Aleppo city
AP II. *See* Additional Protocol II
armed conflict laws, 59, 65n38
al-Assad, Bashar: barrel bombs denied by, 13, 43n20; ceasefires as peace and, 104; on cleansing Aleppo, 81; military attacks by, 72, 102–103; on pushing resistance to Turkey, 104; reconstruction assistance ask by, 86;

regime of, 2–3
Assad government: accountability and civilians killed by, 110; air force used by, 12–14, 42n9; Alawites as for, 34; Aleppo bombed by, 31, 81; Aleppo with opposition and, 30, 81; arrests during displacements and, 29; assembly limited by, 1; attacks not stopped by, 72, 102–103; barrel bombs used by, 42n13–43n14, 43n20, 44n25; ceasefire violated by, 5–6; citizen homogenization plans of, 21, 47n65; civilian numbers manipulated by, 99–100; Darayya siege by, 58–59, 60, 70, 79–80; Decree No.12 of 2016 by, 38; Decree No. 66 of 2012 by, 38; de-escalation and redeployment by, 102; de-escalation zones ambiguity for, 102; demography changed by, 18–19, 26, 46n51, 80, 82, 85–86; demography control by, 40; executions by, 32–33; forced evacuations by, 82; forces fighting for, 55; gender crimes by, 25; Ghouta control by, 46n44; IHL and non-international conflict of, 56; international pressure curbed by, 99; Iran supporting, 28, 34, 55, 56, 72, 82, 101, 104; Level 1 siege used by, 17; local ceasefires benefitting, 92; looting and forces of, 80; military power focus by, 22; militias of, 21–22; opposition

121

Ghouta ceasefire, 17, 45n42, 46n44; international courts blocked by, 6–7; killings and safe passages of, 31; "reconciliation agreements" by, 28; role of, 5–6; for Shiite crescent, 34, 51n131; "Useful Syria" term by, 34
Rwanda, 21

Sarajevo, 69–71, 72, 73, 74, 75
Sarin gas attacks, 3
Scud ballistic missiles, 6
sectarian cleansing: Assad for, 104; crimes and, 20–26; in Damascus suburbs, 94; demography changed by, 20; demography for, 12–13, 34–35, 51n131; gender crimes as, 21; Homs and, 79, 92; looting as, 93; massacres in, 24, 47n70; of Moadamiya, 96; terrorism as, 24–25, 48n87. *See also* massacres
Shabiha forces: civilians joining, 15, 21–22; massacre committed by, 23–24; *Ta'feesh* for rewarding, 27, 49n95, 49n97
Shia: Assad placing, 93; Darayya settled with, 34, 80; Homs settled with, 79, 93; new temples for, 34; Russia, Syria, Iran, Iraq for crescent of, 34, 51n131; Sunnis versus, 24–25
siege: on Aleppo, 62, 81; by Assad government, 15, 16; Assad using Level 1, 17; of Baba Amr, 48n77; ceasefires for reinstating, 94; children influenced by, 45n40; civilian impact by, 74–75; on Damascus suburbs, 94; of Darayya, 58–59, 60, 70, 79–80; definition of, 14; euphemisms of, 46n56; for forced displacements, 28, 84; forced evacuations after, 78; of Ghouta, 17–18; Ghouta city and, 82; of Homs city, 48n77, 78–79, 92; levels of, 15–16, 17; Madaya and starvation of, 98; military tactics of, 70–71; on Moadamiya, 94, 95–96; opposition destroyed with, 18, 46n45; by opposition parties, 15, 16; opposition using Level 3, 17; resistance destroyed by, 18, 46n45; as terrorism, 15; UN not considering, 19, 99; UNSC on, 16,

19–20, 46n56; victim numbers of, 17, 18; al-Waer and lasting, 97; war by, 14–20; as weapon, 14–15; on Yarmouk, Babbila, 95
SNHR. *See* Syrian Network for Human Rights
Somalia civil war, 12, 42n11
statistical analysis: for accountability, 110–111; on anonymous victims, 117–118; arrests, detention numbers and, 1; *bias* as variable coverage rate and, 113; civilian death estimations in, 2, 109–110; civilians death data in, 113–115; data amounts and conclusions in, 113–114; data types and collection, 114; death patterns from, 111; duplicate records identified in, 115–118, 117; for historical record and patterns, 118; on Mayan deaths, 109; MSE and data in, 114–115; observed and unobserved violence in, 111–112; probabilistic matching in, 117; record linkages and, 115; records on civilians and, 115–116; Syrians identified for, 116, 117; Syria with speed and data detail for, 112; unobserved violence accounted by, 111; of violence, 1–2, 109, 111–112
Sunnis, 22–25, 26, 93
"surrender or starve" campaigns: on Aleppo, 101; by Assad government, 14, 15, 77, 80, 82, 84, 86, 99; on Damascus, 94–96; Darayya under, 77, 80
Syria. *See specific subjects*
Syrian Network for Human Rights (SNHR), 2, 112, 114

Ta'feesh, 27, 49n95, 49n97
terrorism: ISIS as, 22, 56, 73; rape as, 25–26; as sectarian cleansing, 24–25, 48n87; siege by, 15
transitional justice programs, 1
Turkey, 5, 32, 72, 73, 101, 104

UDHR. *See* Universal Declaration of Human Rights
UN. *See* United Nations
UN General Assembly (UNGA), 6, 7
UN High Commissioner for Human Rights (UNHCR), 11, 29, 83, 109

United Nations (UN): aid convoys
blocked, 4, 30, 58, 74, 78, 80, 94, 96,
98, 99; aid demand and, 16, 17, 41n3,
45n42, 101; aid lack by, 30, 99, 100,
101; Assad government curbing, 99;
Assad government encouraged by, 99,
100–101; Assad strengthened by, 103;
ceasefires manipulating, 100–101;
civilian numbers manipulated by,
99–100; culpability of, 98–101;
Darayya not helped by, 3–4, 14, 44n25,
80; on evacuations as displacements,
33, 83; hybrid courts supervised by, 7;
The Pinheiro Principles of, 26, 49n92;
siege not considered by, 19, 99
United States (US): FSA supported by, 56;
ISIS focus by, 73; local ceasefires
favored by, 91; moderate rebels backed
by, 4–5; opposition parties and support
by, 55–56
Universal Declaration of Human Rights
(UDHR), 61
unnecessary suffering, 59, 65n44
UN Security Council (UNSC): on besieged
areas, 16; on civilians and siege, 19–20,
46n56; Resolution 2139/2014 of, 14,
19; Resolution 2268 of, 16; Resolution

2401 of, 17; resolution against barrel
bombs, 14; Russia on Ghouta ceasefire
and, 17, 45n42, 46n44
uprising: beginning of, 2; civilian numbers
killed in, ix, 1, 2, 6, 11, 13, 21, 41n6,
43n19, 47n66, 58, 81. *See also*
opposition parties
US. *See* United States
"Useful Syria", 34

violence: anonymous victims of, 117–118;
individuals and records on, 113,
115–116, 117–118; as observed and
unobserved, 111–112; political
transition after end of, ix; rape as
terrorism, 25–26; statistical analysis of,
1–2, 109, 111–112; Syria and history
of, 1–2; victims not collected and, 113

Wadi Barada, 96, 97, 98, 103
al-Waer neighborhood, 5, 28–29, 79, 96,
97, 103
western Aleppo city, 30, 81

Yarmouk, 19, 33, 94, 95

Zadabani, 98

About the Author and Contributors

Radwan Ziadeh is senior fellow at the Arab Center Washington DC (www.arabcenterdc.org) and visiting researcher at the Democratic Transition Program at the Arab Center for Research and Policy Studies in Doha, Qatar. He is also the founder and director of the Damascus Center for Human Rights Studies in Syria (www.dchrs.org) and cofounder and executive director of the Syrian Center for Political and Strategic Studies in Washington, DC (www.scpss.org).

He was the managing editor of the Transitional Justice Project in the Arab World and the head of the Syrian Commission for Transitional Justice, which was established on November 14, 2013, by the Syrian Opposition Interim Government. The Commission was tasked to work on the transitional justice file, including investigating crimes, considering means for prosecution, and building a national reconciliation program, among other items. Since the Syrian uprising started in March 15, 2011, he has been involved in documenting the ongoing human rights violations in Syria. He has testified at the UN Human Rights Council in Geneva twice and in front of the Tom Lantos Human Rights Commission in the U.S. Congress.

He was also involved in the Syrian political opposition. He was elected in October 2011 as director of the Foreign Relations Office of the Syrian National Council until he resigned from the position in November 2012. He has written more than thirty books in English and Arabic, his most recent being *Power and Policy in Syria: Intelligence Services, Foreign Relations and Democracy in the Modern Middle East* (2011) and *The Kurds in Syria: Fueling Separatist Movements in the Region?* (2009).

* * *

David M. Crane is a professor at Syracuse University College of Law and former chief prosecutor of the international war crimes tribunal in West Africa, called the Special Court for Sierra Leone.

Mai El-Sadany is a legal associate at the International Center for Not-For-Profit Law and a non-resident fellow for legal and judicial analysis at the Tahrir Institute for Middle East Policy. She is the cofounder of the Syria Calendar, a crowd-sourced calendar that collates events happening in solidarity with Syria across the world, and Not A Bystander, a new campaign that seeks to mobilize the everyday citizen in the fight against war crimes and crimes against humanity in Syria. El-Sadany is passionate about working on atrocity documentation and prevention in Syria, legal and constitutional issues in Egypt, and human rights issues across the Middle East more broadly. She holds a JD and certificate in refugees and humanitarian emergencies from the Georgetown University Law Center and a BA in political science from Stanford University.

Janine di Giovanni is author of *The Morning They Came for Us*, award-winning foreign correspondent, and current Middle East editor at *Newsweek*.

Mohamad Alaa Ghanem is senior political adviser, government relations director, and strategist at the Syrian American Council. He is also an Atlantic Council Millennium Fellow and a former professor at the University of Damascus, Syria.

Anita Gohdes is a professor at the Hertie School of Governance in Berlin.

Megan Price is executive director of the Human Rights Data Analysis Group. She designs strategies and methods for statistical analysis of human rights data for projects in a variety of locations including Guatemala, Colombia, and Syria. Her work in Guatemala includes serving as the lead statistician on a project in which she analyzes documents from the National Police Archive; she has also contributed analyses submitted as evidence in two court cases in Guatemala. Her work in Syria includes serving as the lead statistician and author on three reports, commissioned by the Office of the United Nations High Commissioner of Human Rights, on documented deaths in that country. Price is a member of the Technical Advisory Board for the Office of the Prosecutor at the International Criminal Court, on the Board of Directors for Tor, a research fellow at the Carnegie Mellon University Center for Human Rights Science, and the human rights editor for the *Statistical Journal of the International Association for Official Statistics*. She earned her doctorate in biostatistics and a Certificate in Human Rights from the Rollins School of Public Health at Emory University. She also holds a master of science degree and bachelor of science degree in statistics from Case Western Reserve University.

Sophia Slater is a researcher and reporter in the Middle East Bureau of *Newsweek* in Paris.

www.ingramcontent.com/pod-product-compliance
Lightning Source LLC
Chambersburg PA
CBHW022325280326
41932CB00010B/1225